Praying with
Passionate Women

Praying with Passionate Women

MYSTICS, MARTYRS, AND MENTORS

Bridget Mary Meehan

CROSSROAD · NEW YORK

1995

The Crossroad Publishing Company
370 Lexington Avenue, New York, NY 10017

Copyright © 1995 by Bridget Mary Meehan

Printed in the United States of America

Library of Congress Cataloging-in-Publication Data

Meehan, Bridget.
    Praying with passionate women : mystics, martyrs, and mentors /
Bridget Mary Meehan.
       p.   cm.
    Includes bibliographical references.
    ISBN 0-8245-1477-7 (pbk.)
    1. Christian women — Biography.   2. Christian women — Religious
life.   3. Prayer — Christianity.   I. Title.
BR1713.M44   1995
270'.092'2–dc20
[B]   95-3889
                                          CIP

To my family:

my parents, Bridie and Jack, my Aunt Molly McCarthy,
my brothers Patrick and Sean, my sisters-in-law Valerie and Nancy,
my niece and nephew Katie and Danny.

To all the women whose strength and compassion
have reflected to me the love of God as Sister and Friend:

especially Regina Madonna Oliver, Mary Emma Haddrick, Jill Hines,
Peg Bowen, Donna Mogan, Kathleen Wiesberg, Olga Gane,
Eugenia Garrido, Irene Marshall, Elizabeth Hoisington, Rosemary Walsh,
Phyllis Hurst, Mary Patricia Mulhall, Evelyn Mulhall, Ruth Reilly,
Kathleen Mulhall, Mary and Megan Fitzgibbons, Jutta Clark,
Alicia Clark, Mary Jo Grotenrath, Estelle Spachman, Debbie Dubuque,
Eileen Kelly, Betsy Hendricks, Bessie Jones, Sandra Voelker,
the Society of Sisters for the Church, and the Sisters for
Christian Community.

To all Celtic women in my family:

Noreen Davy, Molly Meehan, Mary Ferns, Peg Meehan, Mary Tregent,
Margaret Ryan, Mary D. Meehan, Eileen Meehan,
Kathleen McNamara, Esther Meehan, Tess Murphy, Mary Meehan,
Alice Meehan, Elizabeth Murphy, Catherine Murphy, Rose Meehan,
Katherine Meehan, Miriam Meehan, and Eileen Preston.

To Mary, mother of Jesus and mother of the church, whose companionship
reflects sisterly love in the power of Sophia-God.

To all our foremothers in the faith: Mystics, Martyrs, and Mentors.

To all passionate women who live and love as courageous disciples
of Jesus in the contemporary world.

Contents

7

Acknowledgments

In writing this book, I am grateful to my family and friends. The gift of their faith and friendship has touched me deeply.

I am especially thankful to my parents, Bridie and Jack Meehan, who taught me so much about God's love by their love for me. I am also grateful to my Aunt Molly McCarthy, my brothers and sisters-in-law, Patrick and Val, Sean and Nancy, my niece and nephew, Katie and Danny. Their generosity, goodness, and kindness are a constant source of strength and inspiration to me.

I owe a special debt of gratitude to the following friends who have encouraged me along the way: Regina Madonna Oliver, Irene Marshall, Sully and Daisy Sullivan, Jeanette Kraska, Bob Bowen, Ralph E. Stronoski, Bruce Burslie, Millie Nash, Fritz and Barbara Warren, Marie and Steve Billick, Denis and Sue Wenzel, Floyd and Glenda Sullivan, Andrew Malloy, Jesús Campos, Pam Douglas, Marie and Bill Dillon, Francis L. Keete, Eunice Lopez, Leo Schulten, Jr., Dorothy Vaill, Mike Phinney, Virginia Limón, Virginia VanDerWal, Ana Minassian, Kayo Brown, Juliana Blair, Judy and Frank Dillon, Kermit and Lynn Johnson, Bill and Wanda Graham, Isaac and Glenda McCullough, Michal Morsches, Mary and Dick Guertin, Roseanne Fedorko, Mike Marshall, Helen Groff, Larry Skummer, Cheryl Daichandt, Jack Doyle, Paul and Shirley Hurley, Ellen and Cornelius Coakley, Ron Whalen, Jack Klingenhagen, Mary Kay and John Salomone, Mary Cashmen, Elizabeth and Lester Price, John Mathias, John Weyand, Angela Brown, Andrew Jackson, Bob Schaaf, Vera and Art Cole, Bennie Rossler, Paul Wynants, Patricia Herlihy, Helen Pickrel, Lynn Thompson, Rosetta Johnson, Phil Akers, Doris Mason, Maria Kemp, Joe Mulqueen, Charlie McDonnell, Wayne Schmid, and

Walter Montondon for their loving friendship and loyal support during the years.

I am thankful to Ray and Carol Buchanan, good friends who provided expert advisors on technical computer issues for all my books. I am also grateful to Angela Logan for typing and editing this manuscript.

Acknowledgment is gratefully given for permission to quote from the following:

H. Musurillo, trans., *The Acts of the Christian Martyrs* (Oxford: Clarendon, 1972), by permission of Oxford University Press.

"Pure Desert," in *Selected Poetry of Jessica Powers*, ed. Regina Siegfried and Robert Morneau (Kansas City: Sheed and Ward, 1989).

Jerome, *Life of Paula, 3 Letters*, ed. Philip Schaat, ser. 2, vol. 6 (Grand Rapids: William B. Eerdmans, 1952).

Introduction

Ordinary women throughout the ages have lived passionate, courageous, and holy lives. As martyrs, mystics, and mentors they have led us on new pathways into the mysteries of God. By sharing their experiences of God, they reflect dynamic spiritualities flowing from the heart that transcend the mystery of time and space. Today, their voices call us to dwell in God, to share faith, to search for solidarity, to live in communion with others and creation, to advocate systemic justice, to be risk-takers for the gospel, and, above all, to love passionately!

The women whose powerful testimony, mystical visions, and prophetic insights fill the pages of this book are like a vibrant rainbow reflecting a multicolored magnificent picture of the Christian life. They are not all visionaries or mystics. They are not all martyrs. However, they are all mentors, women who show us by their prayer and witness how to be strong, courageous, just, wise, loving, and faith-filled disciples in our time. Their spirit lives on and energizes us in their prayers and visions. As we celebrate their lives and accompany our sisters in deep prayer, we discover a new sense of bondedness and connectedness with these great women of faith in our tradition that can liberate and empower us to fully live God's love now.

"The blood of martyrs is the seed of faith," a saying many of us recall learning sometime during our years of religious education. But when we encounter heroic Perpetua, activist mother and catechumen, in an overcrowded Carthage jail, feeding her newborn baby at the breast and awaiting her martyrdom with courage, we experience the power of this adage in a new way. Perpetua's faith is a light for us today as we strive to promote gospel values in family and neighborhood. Martyr Irene, who laid down her life rather than turn over the Scriptures to Dulcitius to be burned, reveals

11

the meaning of Christian martyrdom for all ages: "It was almighty God who bade us to love unto death."

Desert mothers — Sarah, Theodora, and Syncletica — provide us with wisdom and insight when struggling with the darkness of sin and evil in our lives and in our world. They remind us that prayer and discipline involve a life-long journey toward growth in holiness and wholeness. There is no reason to fear the temptations that come our way because God's presence is with us to deliver, heal, and transform us.

A close friend of Jerome, the renowned biblical translator of the Vulgate, and a holy woman of the fourth century, Paula shows us the significance of mutuality and partnership in our relationships with others in the faith journey. Jerome's account of her death in his *Life of Paula* emphasizes that death is a blessed passage into the embrace of God's overwhelming love. Our trust in God's love enables us to overcome our fears of death and to live life more fully and freely now.

Dhuoda, Frankish mother, not only offers us unique insights into the spiritual and cultural interests of the Carolingian era, but also sheds light on the inner journey of an outstanding woman and a strong mother who, although separated from her children, wrote a manual on the basics of the Christian faith in order to share her beliefs and values with them.

In the twelfth and thirteenth centuries, the visions of medieval women flourished, and according to Dronke, "It is to women that we owe some of the highest flights of mystical poetry in the Middle Ages."[1] Among the most renowned women of this period are Hildegard of Bingen, Beatrice of Nazareth, Hadewijch of Brabant, Mechtild of Magdeburg, Mechtild of Hackeborn, and Gertrude the Great.

A writer, prophet, preacher, mystic, and visionary, Hildegard dialogued and corresponded with popes, prelates, emperors, lay persons, abbesses, priests, and monks. She was honored and esteemed by Pope Eugene III, Bernard of Clairvaux, and many others within the church. At forty-two, she began her major visionary work *Scivias*, which contained twenty-six visions on such topics as the love of God for humanity in creation, salvation, the

Trinity, and the church. Each of her visions is described with vivid imagery and brilliant colors. Hildegard's vision of the cosmos and creation draws us into profound adoration and deep awe as stewards of creation.

Beatrice of Nazareth, a thirteenth-century visionary Cistercian, wrote a mystical treatise called *The Seven Steps of Love*, which outlines the stages of development in our love of God. According to her plan for interior growth, we begin with a desire to serve God and reflect on our motives and desires to love more deeply, then continue on the spiritual path discovering total freedom and deep love. Beatrice's timeless counsel assures us that no matter what our difficulties and trials in life, God's love will prevail.

Often referred to as "the Brabant Mystic" because the dialect in which she wrote was that of the lower Rhenish city of Brabant, Hadewijch, scholars tell us, used images of courtly love in her writings to describe her mystic experiences. Her writings open us to new insights into the power of human love to reveal the Holy One in our midst. Her words echo in the hearts of lovers in every century: "Love's burning desire is a precious gift; the lover knows this and asks no more."[2]

Mechtild of Magdeburg, a member of the Beguines, whose members lived in female communities and gathered together to share spiritual insights, imaged God as a loving mother who created women and men in the divine image. Unafraid to speak out against the abuses of clerics and the injustices in the church, Mechtild is a companion to women today who are calling their churches to expand their images of God in order to understand the God beyond male and female, and to all those who challenge patriarchy and its accompanying sexism within the church.

Believing that God's infinite love was beyond all comprehension for those she loved, Mechtild of Hackeborn is a source of encouragement to us as we grow in intimacy with others and as we face changes, transitions, stress, or loss in these relationships. In one such revelation, which she shared with Gertrude the Great, Mechtild observes: "In the light of eternal truth I now see clearly that all my love for those who were dear to me in this life is no more than a drop in the ocean in comparison with the love of the Sacred Heart for them."[3]

Gertrude the Great's devotion to the Sacred Heart of Jesus symbolizes the heart of Jesus as "the bond or bridge between his humanity and his divinity." One of Gertrude's visions describes a "stream breaking forth from the Heart of Jesus, which appeared to water all the place where she was. She understood that this stream was the efficacy of the prayers which she offered at His feet." Gertrude's image of the Heart of Jesus has become a popular symbol that offers comfort and healing, reminding us that God is always loving us at every moment of our lives.[4]

Four women mystics in medieval Italy speak powerfully to our contemporary society as we approach the threshold of a new millennium: Clare of Assisi, Angela of Foligno, Catherine of Siena, and Catherine of Genoa.

Born into a prosperous family in 1194 in Assisi, Clare, in solidarity with her friend Francis of Assisi, chose a life of poverty and contemplative prayer. Clare is a role model for Christians today who are simplifying their lifestyles and living as midwives to a New Earth. Contemplation, in the spirit of Clare, leads to action on behalf of the poor.

Angela of Foligno is portrayed by her biographers as intelligent, well-educated, a married socialite who "colored and braided" her hair and wore shoes "adorned with cut leather." Angela certainly seems to fit the image of a fashion conscious, attractive woman of her time. After a sudden conversion experience, Angela joined the Franciscan Tertiaries, a small faith community dedicated to living according to the spirit of St. Francis of Assisi. Describing the mystical life in a sequence of seven steps, Angela's visions reveal God's presence in spiritual darkness. Her words give comfort during times of sadness, discouragement, and depression.

The second youngest of twenty-five children, Catherine of Siena was born in the Italian city of Siena. She became a member of a group of laywomen associated with the Dominican order at the age of sixteen and lived in solitude in a small room in her parents' house. There she experienced a mystical marriage with Christ, and, in response to God's call, Catherine began a ministry to the poor and needy of Siena. In a church filled with political and social tension, she preached reform. As a mystic activist, Catherine is a mentor to women and men in the church today who struggle for the transformation of both church and society to be more inclusive, whole, and holy.

Caterina Adorna, better known as Catherine of Genoa, lived in the fifteenth-century Italian seaport of Genoa. A married woman and an administrator of a large city hospital, Catherine was known for mystical visions and her care for the needy. In the hospital where she worked, Catherine sought solitude in a small room where she could pray and be "wholly absorbed in secret delights." On some occasions she was found there, lying still, "like one dead," her face buried in her hands. However, her biographer comments, if anyone called her in need she would respond quickly, "with a glowing countenance, like a cherub." Catherine is an icon for contemporary women who love their husbands, children, careers, and communities and are serious about their inner journey.[5]

Two very different women stand out as models of female spirituality in the fourteenth century: Marguerite d'Oingt and Julian of Norwich. Little biographical information is available about either of them. Joining the Carthusians, a contemplative religious order, Marguerite became the fourth prioress of the community at Poleteins in France. In contrast, Julian was an anchoress, who lived alone in a small room attached to the church of St. Julian in Norwich, England. However, both these women were writers who shared their experiences about the spiritual life. Both described the feminine face of God and the motherhood of Christ. Marguerite did not desire to have any mother or father except Christ. She wondered if Christ was not more than her mother, since her mother labored to give her birth in a single day or night, but Christ labored to give her spiritual life for more than thirty years.[6] Julian, who is perhaps best known for her writings on the motherhood of God, described God's mothering activity in her *Revelations of Divine Love*. "As truly as God is our Father, so truly is God our mother," Julian reminds us.[7] With these two women mystics we are invited to pray with feminine images of God and to participate in the discussion of one of the major theological issues facing the church today: the God-question.

Women mentors, like Teresa of Avila, Jane Frances de Chantal, Mary Ward, Elizabeth Bayley Seton, and Thérèse of Lisieux, who share the deepest truths of their existence, their spiritual history, and the visions of God, deepen our understanding of the role that ordinary women play as instruments of God's plan. As living models of God's passionate love, these women show us by word and example how to open ourselves to the divine indwelling presence within us and within all creation.

The renowned Spanish mystic Teresa of Avila reformed the Carmelite order and wrote extensively about the spiritual life. In *The Interior Castle*, one of her popular works, Teresa uses the image of a mansion as a symbol of the stages in spiritual growth. Each mansion has several rooms through which the soul moves to encounter the king. The bottom line, Teresa tells us, is "the more advanced you are in love for your neighbor the more advanced you will be in love for God." It is pretty hard to beat this solid advice for spiritual living today.

Jeanne-Françoise de Chantal was a wealthy and happily married woman and mother of seven children when her husband was killed in a hunting accident. Jane coped with the loss and difficulties of raising her children in her in-laws' home. Her approach to life was characterized by gentleness. In a world where stress and pressure are often the norm, Jane reminds us to be gentle with ourselves, relax, breathe deeply, and "put yourself very simply before God, certain of his presence everywhere, and without any effort, whisper very softly … whatever your heart prompts you to say."[8]

Like Mary Ward and her followers, contemporary religious orders are still dealing with new questions and developing new roles for women in religious life. "Stretching the institution," Benedictine sister Joan Chittister reminds us, is the prophetic role of religious who are "the wake-up call of the church."[9] Mary Ward, founder of the Institute of the Blessed Virgin Mary, the first unenclosed order for active women religious in the Roman Catholic Church, challenged an old institution to adapt itself to a changing world. In an age whose only concept of religious life for women was enclosure in a monastery or convent, church officials did not want women on the streets feeding the hungry, comforting the sick, or doing anything outside the cloister. Undaunted by the harsh criticism of her detractors, Mary Ward believed in the dream that women today continue to dream: "And I hope in God it will be seen that women in time will do much."[10]

A convert to Catholicism, Elizabeth Bayley Seton overcame the tragic death of her young husband and the deaths of her two children, along with the loss of the family fortune. In 1808 Elizabeth moved to Baltimore, and in 1809, with four other women, she founded the American Sisters of Charity and the first American Catholic school. At the time of her death in 1821 at age forty-six in Emmitsburg, Maryland, her new congregation numbered twenty communities in the United States. On September 14, 1975, Elizabeth Bayley Seton — wife, mother, widow, foundress — was declared America's first native-born Roman Catholic saint. As our national role model, Elizabeth reminds us of the things that really matter in life — faith, courage, determination, and love.

The ninth child of Louis Martin and Zelie Guerin, Thérèse of Lisieux was born in the town of Alençon in France on January 2, 1873. She was brought up in a loving, close-knit family. At fifteen, Thérèse entered the Carmelite convent at Lisieux. Describing this day, Thérèse tells us, "My soul experienced a peace so sweet and so deep, it would be impossible to express it" (Story, 148).[11] Her approach to spirituality has touched the hearts of people throughout the world from different cultures and traditions and continues to be popular today. In The Story of a Soul Thérèse describes her "little way": "Instead of becoming discouraged, I said to myself: God cannot inspire unrealizable desires. I can, then, in spite of my littleness, aspire to holiness. It is impossible for me to grow up, and so I must bear with myself such as I am with all my imperfections. But I want to seek out a means of going to heaven by a little way, a way that is very straight, very short, and totally new" (Story, 207).

At the heart of our spiritual journey in this century we find the realism of Evelyn Underhill, the wisdom of Edith Stein, the prophetic courage of Dorothy Day, the wholistic spirituality of Caryll Houselander, the powerful poetry of Jessica Powers, a martyr for justice, Ita Ford, and the strength of civil rights activist Rosa Parks.

Born into a prominent family in England in the late nineteenth century, Evelyn Underhill grew up in an agnostic environment. At the age of thirty-two Evelyn had a profound religious conversion experience that convinced her of the truth of the Catholic faith. When the church condemned Modernism, which she believed in, she chose to follow her own inner wisdom and did not become a member of the Roman Catholic Church. In 1911, she wrote *Mysticism*, a classical work on religious experience that is still popular today. Evelyn became a twentieth-century mystic whose prayer finds the holy in the real world of unpaid bills, aging parents, traffic jams, stressful schedules, unruly children, demanding jobs. "Lay your sacred hands on all the common things and small interests of that life and bless and change them. Transfigure my small resources, make them sacred. And in them give me your very self."[12]

The youngest of eleven children, Edith Stein was born into a devout Jewish family on October 12, 1891. After finishing her doctoral studies Edith decided to give lectures, becoming a well-known speaker in Germany, Switzerland, and Austria. For Edith, Teresa of Avila's *Life* was a profound touchstone that led her to understanding and insight into the spiritual journey. As a result she was baptized on January 1, 1922, and eleven years later entered Carmel. In 1942, Edith was captured by the Nazis. A victim of the Holocaust, she was put to death in the gas chamber of Auschwitz on August 9, 1942. As an intellectual and visionary, Edith Stein left behind a rich legacy of philosophical work and an understanding of women that surpassed role stereotypes.

Dorothy Day — prophet, social activist, contemplative-in-action — lived the gospel of Jesus among the poor and outcast members of society. With Peter Maurin, Dorothy founded the Catholic Worker Movement, an organization dedicated to collaborative decision-making and to personal activism on behalf of workers. For Dorothy and the Catholic Worker Movement, gospel witness meant not only serving the poor but also living in solidarity with the poor and oppressed people of the world. Today we need her courage more than ever as we seek to serve the poor, heal the earth, live in peace, and work for systemic justice.

Calling herself a "rocking horse" Catholic because she became a member of the church at the age of six, Caryll Houselander was an English mystic and popular spiritual writer in the twentieth century who reminds us that we can pray with our hands, our bodies, our whole being and that everything, even our cat, can be our spiritual director. This is certainly fitting advice for all of us who seek a wholistic approach to life and spirituality and who are developing a new earth consciousness that emphasizes our connectedness with self and our family of creatures.

Jessica Powers, the third child of Irish immigrants John and Delia Powers, was born on February 7, 1905. She grew up in rural Wisconsin. In 1937, her first book of poetry, *The Lantern Burns*, was published. She decided to become a contemplative and entered the Milwaukee Carmel in 1941. Jessica wrote close to four hundred poems. In her poem "Pure Desert," she describes the struggle a person might encounter in prayer. Her vivid imagery and rich symbols give us marvelous insights into the sufferings and joys of the spiritual desert that we too may experience.

> I coax you onward: soon, first breeze of bliss;
> soon, sun that scorches cooled to sun that warms.
> Your youth will dance when shady lanes lock arms
> with each green oasis.[13]

On a deserted road in El Salvador in 1980, Maryknoll sisters Ita Ford and Maura Clark, Ursuline Sister Dorothy Kazel, and missionary Jean Donovan were murdered by the National Guard. Chilling pictures of the four women's brutalized bodies appeared on TV and in the newspapers around the world. Outrage and disbelief at this heinous crime followed. The legacy of Ita Ford and her companions challenges us today to work for justice and peace locally and globally. Ita Ford's words will live in our hearts and minds forever as a rich source of inspiration and renewal in our commitment to work for peace and justice in our world. "All I can share with you is that God's palpable presence has never been more real ever since we came to Salvador."[14]

Rosa Parks was born in Tuskegee, Alabama, on February 4, 1913. During her childhood and young adulthood, discrimination against African Americans was widespread. "Jim Crow" laws dictated that blacks had to be separated from whites in public places. On Thursday, December 1, 1955, Rosa got on a bus to return home from work. She recognized the driver. It was James Blake, the man who in 1943 had driven away and left her standing on the sidewalk when she had dared to defy his order by walking through the front of the bus — an action forbidden to blacks at that time.

"Y'all make it light on yourselves and let me have those seats," Blake said. The other blacks in the row stood up, but Rosa did not move. She decided that it was unjust to be forced to give up her seat after she had paid her fare like the white people. Blake called the police. Rosa was arrested and put in jail. African Americans in Montgomery then decided that they would not ride the buses until this discriminatory law was changed. Her courageous decision not to give up her bus seat to a white man and her arrest for breaking the city's segregation law were the first steps of the historic black civil rights movement. Rosa's actions changed our history in this country and earned her the title "Mother of the Civil Rights Movement."[15]

Praying with Passionate Women invites you to experience the power of God's love revealed in the lives of women in the Christian tradition. Each of the prayer experiences begins with introductory material, providing you with a brief background on the lives of these vibrant foremothers of the faith. After that you will find a reflection from their life or writings, four discussion questions, and seven suggestions for prayer to help you contemplate the depths of divine love that these mystics, martyrs, and mentors reveal for your spiritual journey. Open yourself to women wisdom, women liberation, women courage, women strength, and women passion. Dialogue with these models for contemplation. Question these icons of the tradition. Argue with these prophetic witnesses to the gospel. Establish a relationship with these visionaries and guides. They are our sisters. Realize that their stories are also our stories. Their spirits stir up our energies, invite our response, seek our involvement. Share your ideas, experiences, hopes, frustrations, and dreams with these soul companions. As you do so, be aware of the images, feelings, insights, and sensations that emerge.

In the prayer experiences, I recommend that you use a variety of approaches to contemplate their feminine insights and spiritual encounters. Some possibilities are: journaling, poetry, dance, body movement, mime, drama, song, or some artistic forms like drawing, painting, sculpting, playing with clay, or needlepoint. You may wish to use all or some of the prayer suggestions provided in each prayer experience as a guided meditation, or to skip around, trying a different one each time you pray with these passionate women. Listen to your subconscious and try what attracts or excites you. Be conscious of what nourishes your creative spirit and do that!

Groups could use one or more of the discussion questions to get people talking about the contributions of these dynamic women and their impact on our lives and hearts. Background music may provide an appropriate setting for reflection and sharing. Use classical or instrumental music. Before beginning, the group should decide on a facilitator to lead the guided prayer for the group and organize materials and space for art, journaling, story, body movement, creative activity, and so forth. After everything is ready, the facilitator reads aloud one or more of the prayer experiences, then allows time for reflection and response. Groups could then share their experiences and/or their responses to the discussion starters. Larger groups could break into groups of five or six for the discussion.

Praying with Passionate Women introduces women — as well as men — to great women in the Christian tradition who nurtured and shaped spirituality through the ages. It invites individuals

and groups to experience in their own lives the power, love, enthusiasm, wisdom, and courage of passionate women — mystics,
martyrs, and mentors. This book hopes to make their visions
accessible for contemporary Christians. Their female voices and
writings offer opportunities for deep encounters with divine love
and provide support for prophetic witness in the inbreaking of
God's reign in our midst.

Praying with
Passionate Women

Perpetua

(d. March 7, 202)

Introduction

Perpetua, a newly married woman from a prominent family, was among the catechumens arrested and imprisoned for being a Christian in Carthage, North Africa, in 202. In prison, Perpetua had powerful dreams and visions in which she fought the power of evil and won. Perpetua described her dream-vision of triumph over the Devil in the following passage:

> The day before we were to fight with the beast I saw the following vision. Pomponius, the deacon, came to the prison gates and began to knock violently. I went out and opened the gate for him. He was dressed in an unbelted white tunic, wearing elaborate sandals. And he said to me: Perpetua, come; we are waiting for you.
>
> Then he took my hand and we began to walk through rough and broken country. At last we came to the amphitheatre out of breath, and he led me into the centre of the arena.
>
> Then he told me: "Do not be afraid. I am here struggling with you." Then he left.
>
> I looked at the enormous crowd who watched in astonishment. I was surprised that no beasts were let loose on me; for I knew that I was condemned to die by the beasts. Then out came an Egyptian against me, of vicious appearance, together with his seconds, to fight with me. There also came up to me some handsome young men to be my seconds and assistants....
>
> We drew close to one another and began to let our fists fly. My opponent tried to get hold of my feet. Then I was

raised up into the air and I began to pummel him without as it were touching the ground. Then when I noticed there was a lull, I put my two hands together linking the fingers of one hand with those of the other and thus I got hold of his head. He fell flat on his face and I stepped on his head.

The crowd began to shout and my assistants started to sing psalms. Then I walked up to the trainer and took the branch. He kissed me and said to me: "Peace be with you, my daughter!" I began to walk in triumph towards the Gate of Life. Then I awoke. I realized that it was not with wild animals that I would fight but with the Devil, but I knew that I would win the victory.[1]

Perpetua demonstrated remarkable courage throughout her imprisonment and up to the day of her martyrdom, when she was killed by the sword. The *Acts of Perpetua and Felicitas* describe her violent death:

She screamed as she was struck on the bone; then she took the trembling hand of the young gladiator and guided it to her throat. It was as though so great a woman, feared as she was by the unclean spirit, could not be dispatched unless she herself were willing.[2]

Reflection

The anxieties and difficulties Perpetua faced in prison as a nursing mother with her infant son at the breast are described in the following passage:

A number of young catechumens were arrested, Revocatus and his fellow slave Felicitas, Saturninus and Secundulus, and with them Vivia Perpetua, a newly married woman of good family and upbringing. Her mother and father were still alive and one of her two brothers was a catechumen like herself. She was about twenty-two years old and had an infant son at the breast. (Now from this point on the entire account of her [Perpetua's] ordeal is her own according to her own ideas and in the way that she herself wrote it down.)

While we were still under arrest (she said), my father out of love for me was trying to persuade me and shake my resolution. "Father," said I, "do you see this vase here, for example, or waterpot or whatever?"

"Yes, I do," said he.

And I told him: "Could it be called by any other name than what it is?"

And he said: "No."

Well, so, too, I cannot be called anything other than what I am, a Christian."

At this my father was so angered by the word "Christian" that he moved towards me as though he would pluck my eyes out. But he left it at that and departed, vanquished along with his diabolical arguments.

For a few days afterwards I gave thanks to the Lord that I was separated from my father, and I was comforted by his absence.

During these few days I was baptized, and I was inspired by the spirit not to ask for any other favour after the water but simply the perseverance of the flesh. A few days later we were lodged in the prison; and I was terrified, as I had never before been in such a dark hole. What a difficult time it was! With the crowd, the heat was stifling; then there was the extortion of the soldiers; and to crown all, I was tortured with worry for my baby there.

Then Tertius and Pomponius, those blessed deacons who tried to take care of us, bribed the soldiers to allow us to go to a better part of the prison to refresh ourselves for a few hours. All then left that dungeon and shifted for themselves. I nursed my baby, who was faint from hunger. In my anxiety I spoke to my mother about the child, I tried to comfort my brother, and I gave the child into their charge. I was in pain because I saw them suffering out of pity for me. These were the trials I had to endure for many days. Then I got permission for my baby to stay with me in prison. At once I recovered my health, relieved as I was of my worry and anxiety over the child. My prison had suddenly become a palace, so that I wanted to be there rather than anywhere else.[3]

Discussion Starters

1. How is Perpetua a model of courage and faith for Christians today? How is Perpetua's faithfulness to the gospel and willingness to suffer for Christ a source of encouragement for all those who face persecution, violence, discrimination, abuse, or violation of human rights in our world today?

2. In what ways do you experience the struggle between good and evil? In what ways does our contemporary church and world experience this struggle? Who are our contemporary martyrs?

3. Perpetua is an activist mother, fighting for the health, safety, and well-being of her baby. What similar struggles do mothers today face?

4. How does the response of Perpetua to suffering and death give you strength in your daily struggles and trials?

Prayer Experience

1. Spend a little time in stillness. Close your eyes. Relax all your muscles from your head to your toes, or tighten your muscles one by one and then relax them. Take several slow, deep breaths. Be aware of God's loving presence.

2. Read the reflection above, from *Acts of Perpetua and Felicitas* 2–3, slowly and meditatively.

3. Imagine that you are present when Perpetua and the catechumens were arrested and put in prison. Be aware of the fear and discomfort they faced leaving the security of their homes and faith communities...the hardship and pain of their families...the loneliness and sadness they felt. Listen to the conversation between Perpetua and her father. Be aware of their feelings...anger...frustration...hurt...relief. Observe the joy of Perpetua as she is baptized...her anxiety as a young mother over her baby's health and well-being...her concern for her brother and mother...her joy as she nursed her baby

at the breast in prison...her deep faith in the gospel...her courage to suffer martyrdom for Christ.

4. Conduct a dialogue with Perpetua. Ask her questions. Listen to her response. Share your thoughts, feelings, fears, struggles, joys, victories, and faith journey with her.

5. Pray for parents, especially young mothers today who encounter difficulties raising their children. Ask Perpetua, activist mother, to intercede for the health, safety, and well-being of all children and families, especially those who suffer poverty, neglect, abuse, violence, hunger.

6. Reflect on a time when you faced a major struggle or temptation in your spiritual journey. Be aware of how you experienced the presence of darkness or evil in your struggle. Remember how you experienced God's power in this situation. Write a prayer of thanksgiving for whatever God did to strengthen you during this time.

7. Consider how God is calling you to deeper faith and greater courage in your life now. Reflect on your choices. Ask God to give you the wisdom to discern the divine direction for your life. Decide on a plan for spiritual growth that you will try. Record this plan as well as any feelings, thoughts, insights, or images that emerge during your discernment process in your prayer journal.

Irene

(d. April 1, 304)

Introduction

Irene and her companions Agape and Chione were from Thessalonica. Attempting to flee the persecution of Diocletian and Maximian, they were captured and condemned to die. One of Irene's crimes was concealing Christian books (probably the Scriptures) in defiance of the emperor's order to turn them over for burning. Scholars believe that this may indicate that she held a position of leadership in the church.

> When the persecution was raging under the Emperor Maximian, these women, who had adorned themselves with virtue, following the precepts of the gospel, abandoned their native city, their family, property, and possessions because of their love of God and their expectation of heavenly things, performing deeds worthy of their father Abraham. They fled the persecutors, according to the commandment, and took refuge on a high mountain. There they gave themselves to prayer; though their bodies resided on a mountain top, their souls lived in heaven.[1]

> Irene was questioned by authorities and was sentenced to be placed naked in a brothel.

> After those who were put in charge had taken the girl off to the public brothel in accordance with the prefect's order, by the grace of the Holy Spirit which preserved and guarded her pure and inviolate for the God who is the lord of all things, no man dared to approach her or so much as tried to insult her in her speech. Hence the prefect Dulcitius called back this most saintly girl, had her stand before the tribunal, and said to her, "Do you still persist in the same folly?"

But Irene said to him, "It is not folly, but piety."

He then asked for a sheet of papyrus and wrote the sentence against her as follows, "Whereas Irene has refused to obey the command of the emperors and to offer sacrifice, and still adheres to a sect called Christians, I therefore sentence her to be burned alive, as I did her two sisters before her."

After this sentence had been pronounced by the prefect, the soldiers took the girl and brought her to a high place, where her sisters had been martyred before her. They ignited a huge pyre and ordered her to climb up on it. And the holy woman Irene, singing and praising God, threw herself upon it and so died. It was in the ninth consulship of Diocletian Augustus, in the eighth of Maximian Augustus [304 C.E.], on the first day of April, in the reign of our Lord Christ Jesus, who reigns for ever, with whom there is glory to God with the Holy Spirit for ever. Amen.[2]

Irene's courageous testimony reflects the independent spirit of the Christian women martyrs of the early church, their strong resistance to political oppression, and their willingness to embrace martyrdom for the sake of the gospel.

Reflection

After the most holy women were consumed in the flames, the saintly Irene was once again brought before the court on the following day. Dulcitius said to her, "It is clear from what we have seen that you are determined in your folly, for you have deliberately kept even till now many tablets, books, parchments, codices, and pages of the writings of the former Christians of unholy name.... You are not satisfied with the punishment of your sister, nor do you keep before your eyes the terror of death. Therefore you must be punished.

"Will you do the bidding of our emperors and Caesars? Are you prepared to eat the sacrificial meats and to sacrifice to the gods?"

"No," said Irene, "I am not prepared, for the sake of the God almighty who 'has created heaven and earth and the seas and all that is

*in them' [Acts 4:24]. For those who transgress the word of God there
awaits great judgement of eternal punishment."*

The prefect Dulcitius said, *"Who was it that advised you to retain
those parchments and writings up to the present time?"*

"It was almighty God," said Irene, *"who bade us to love unto death.
For this reason we did not dare to be traitors, but we chose to be burned
alive or suffer anything else that might happen to us rather than betray
the writings."*[3]

Discussion Starters

1. Irene reveals the meaning of Christian martyrdom: "It was
   almighty God who bade us to love unto death." What impact
   does Irene's insight have on your understanding of Christian
   martyrdom?

2. How do contemporary martyrs witness to the gospel (e.g.,
   Archbishop Romero, the sisters who were raped and murdered
   in El Salvador, the Jesuits and their housekeeper who were
   murdered in El Salvador, the thousands of people in Latin
   America, Africa, and throughout the world who have been
   slain for their witness to the gospel)?

3. Irene's commitment to the Scriptures is evident in her willingness to lay down her life rather than turn over the Scriptures
   to Dulcitius to be burned. How can reading and/or praying the
   Scriptures influence your choices and decisions in daily life?

4. The women martyrs of the early Christian community demonstrated a courage drawn from an interior presence. Identifying
   with Christ came in the experience of sharing Christ's sufferings and death. How can our union with Christ in prayer help
   us to overcome our fears and to courageously live the gospel
   in our daily lives?

Prayer Experience

1. Become conscious of your breathing. Allow your breathing to
   relax your body. Try a centering exercise such as focusing on

your breathing, praying a mantra, or repeating a prayer word such as "God," "Jesus," "trust," "love," "peace," "courage," or "faith."

2. Read the accounts of Irene's martyrdom slowly and meditatively, as if you were present with her. Use all your senses to get a picture of the scene. Irene reflected a deep union with Christ and a deep desire to share Christ's sufferings and death. Her union with Christ in prayer helped her to overcome fear and to courageously choose martyrdom for the gospel. Write a description or draw a picture of Irene's ordeal in your prayer journal.

3. Consider how you have laid down your life so that others may experience Christ's love more fully in their lives. Draw a cross and fill it with words or images of your "living witness" to the gospel.

4. The stories, symbols, and images of the Scriptures give us rich possibilities for prayer. Using imagination and visualizations to dialogue with and enter into symbols and stories in the Scriptures can help us encounter God in a deeper and fuller way. Choose a favorite passage from the Bible. Reflect on the Scripture passage in order to discover some new insight or practical application to a specific situation or relationship in your life, for example, "I will espouse you to me forever . . . and you shall know the Lord" (Hos. 2:21, 22). Listen to God express a heartfelt longing for a more intimate relationship with you. The passionate, tender love between spouses is a symbol of God's infinite love for us. Open yourself to the Divine Lover speaking in the depths of your soul. Share your thoughts and feelings with God.

5. Be aware of ways that praying the Scriptures can influence your choices or decisions. In meditation on the Scriptures one asks, "God, what are you saying to me through this passage; or what do you want me to change, choose, and/or do in response to your Word?" In the example given in no. 4, a person could decide to spend more time in quiet prayer listening to God and relaxing in the embrace of infinite love. Decide what

you will choose or do as a response to the Scripture passage you read in no. 4.

6. Be aware of any blockages or bondages that keep you from living the gospel as a committed, passionate disciple of Christ. Imagine God freeing you from any obstacles that keep you from being receptive to God's love ... freeing you from any bondage to sin ... healing your fears and anxieties ... filling you with trust ... courage ... wisdom ... strength ... determination ... perseverance ... patience ... love ... transforming you into a radiant witness of the gospel.

7. The women martyrs of the early Christian community are our foremothers in the faith. Compose your own prayer of intercession or blessing, invoking their help in the events of your life and for the needs of the world. Offer this prayer for courage for self, family, friends, community, neighbors, church, and the world in times of fear, oppression, threat, or danger.

Desert Mother Sarah

(Fifth Century)

Introduction

Amma (Mother) Sarah was one of the desert mothers who probably lived in the fifth century. She may have been a member of one of the new communities of ascetics that emerged at this time. It is not possible to assign dates to the sayings of Sarah or the other desert mothers because they began as oral tradition, were then carefully preserved by disciples, and later put into collections that became known in the West through the scholarship of John Cassian, Jerome, and Palladius. The following passage from desert mother Sarah reflects her wisdom in dealing with the forces of evil. From our foremother Sarah we can learn effective approaches for our struggles with sinful tendencies and temptations in our lives.[1]

Reflection

It was related of Amma Sarah that for thirteen years she waged warfare against the demon of fornication. She never prayed that the warfare should cease but she said, "O God, give me strength."

Once the same spirit of fornication attacked her more intently, reminding her of the vanities of the world. But she gave herself up to the fear of God and to asceticism and went up onto her little terrace to pray. Then the spirit of fornication appeared corporally to her and said, "Sarah, you have overcome me." But she said, "It is not I who have overcome you but my master, Christ."

Amma Sarah said, "If I prayed God that all should approve of my conduct, I should find myself a penitent at the door of each one, but I shall rather pray that my heart may be pure towards all."

She also said, "I put out my foot to ascend the ladder, and I place death before my eyes before going up it."

She also said, "It is good to give alms to those in need. Even if it is only done to please people, through it one can begin to seek to please God."[2]

Discussion Starters

1. What does desert mother Sarah teach us about overcoming temptation?
2. In what ways do you see people throughout the world struggling with the darkness of sin and evil?
3. What are the greatest temptations or sinful tendencies you face in your spiritual journey now? What can you do to overcome these temptations or sinful tendencies?
4. In what ways can your struggles with sinful tendencies help you grow closer to God and to others?

Prayer Experience

1. Become conscious of your breathing. As you breathe deeply, imagine tension leaving each area of your body and relaxation flowing through your body. Say to yourself, "I feel tension leaving my body and relaxation flowing from the top of my head, through my neck, shoulders, back, chest, arms, hands, stomach, hips, legs, feet.
2. Read desert mother Sarah's reflection slowly and thoughtfully.
3. Light a candle in a dark room or imagine a lighted candle glowing in the darkness. Be attentive that God's presence is like the light that shines brightly in the darkness. Be aware of sinful tendencies, temptations, compulsions that you face in your life now. Ask God to forgive, free, heal, and transform you in each of these areas. Observe God leading you out of the darkness of each sinful tendency, temptation, and compulsion into the light of forgiveness, freedom, and healing. Offer thanks for God's saving presence acting powerfully in your life.

4. As you experience God's radiant light in your life now, be aware of any feelings, thoughts, images, insights, or sensations that emerge. Share your feelings with God in a loving conversation. Record these responses in your prayer journal.

5. Be aware of any ways that you can minister to others as a "wounded healer" by sharing your weaknesses and God's saving power in your life with them. Share with God any challenges you think you will encounter as you strive to minister to others in this way. Open yourself to God's grace and allow this grace to fill you with the compassion and courage you need to be a "wounded healer."

6. Pray for people throughout the world who struggle with sin and evil such as wars, ethnic conflicts, poverty, homelessness, discrimination, joblessness, injustice, violence, or abuse. Ask God to comfort and strengthen them in their sufferings and to create a new world in which justice, peace, freedom, equality, and gospel values prevail. Decide on one way you will contribute time, money, or energy to some outreach charitable organization such as Catholic Charities, the Red Cross, Bread for the World, Catholic Near East Welfare Society, or Amnesty International.

7. Compose a mantra or short prayer verse to use during times of temptation. Desert mother Sarah prayed, "O God, give me strength." Draw, paint, or embroider your prayer mantra and put it in a prominent place in your home or work site to remind you of God's saving power in your life.

Desert Mother Theodora

(Fifth Century)

Introduction

Amma (Mother) Theodora was one of the hermits or nuns presumed to have lived in the fifth-century Egyptian desert. Little is known of her life. All we have are these sayings that were preserved by her disciples and eventually became part of the collections of sayings from the desert. Desert mother Theodora's sayings reflect a keen insight into the process of spiritual development. Here the person is addressed in his or her wholeness — body, mind, and spirit. For the Christian, prayer and discipline involve a life-long journey toward growth in holiness and wholeness.[1]

Reflection

Amma Theodora said, "Let us strive to enter by the narrow gate. Just as the trees, if they have not stood before the winter's storms, cannot bear fruit, so it is with us; this present age is a storm and it is only through many trials and temptations that we can obtain an inheritance in the kingdom of heaven."

She also said, "It is good to live in peace, for the wise person practices perpetual prayer. It is truly a great thing for a virgin or a monk to live in peace, especially for the younger ones. However, you should realize that as soon as you intend to live in peace, at once evil comes and weighs down your soul through accidie,[2] faintheartedness, and evil thoughts. It also attacks your body through sickness, debility, weakening of the knees, and all the members. It dissipates the strength of soul and body, so that one believes one is ill and no longer able to pray. But if we are vigilant, all these temptations fall away. There was, in fact, a nun who was seized by cold and fever every time she began to pray, and she suffered from headaches, too. In this condition, she said to herself, 'I am ill, and near to death; so now I will get up before I die and pray.' By reasoning in this way, she did violence to herself and prayed. When she had finished, the fever abated also. So, by reasoning in this way, the sister resisted, and prayed and was able to conquer her thoughts." ...

The same Amma Theodora said, "A devout woman happened to be insulted by someone, and she said to her, 'I could say as much to you, but the commandment of God keeps my mouth shut.'" She also said this, "A Christian discussing the body with a Manichean expressed herself in these words, 'Give the body discipline and you will see that the body is for the one who made it.'"[3]

Discussion Starters

1. In what ways is the Christian life a life-long journey toward holiness and wholeness?

2. How does Theodora address the person in his or her wholeness?

3. How can you reflect a wholistic approach to spiritual growth in your life?

4. In what ways can prayer and discipline help you grow as a healthy and holy person?

Prayer Experience

1. Stand up, stretch, and take several minutes to relax your body by alternately tensing and relaxing each muscle area beginning with your head, face, and neck and ending with your ankles, feet, and toes. Then sit down and breathe in a slow, deep breath, and release it slowly. Keep breathing this way until you feel relaxed.

2. Read desert mother Theodora's reflection in a quiet and leisurely manner.

3. Be aware of any times when you experienced your body as holy and whole...a temple of God's Spirit...an instrument of God's grace...touching others with tenderness...loving and serving the needs of family...friends...neighbors...the community...feeding and clothing the hungry, homeless, and poor...hugging the lonely, depressed, or sad...helping the sick, the suffering, and others. Now look at your body in a mirror or at a picture of yourself. Affirm and give thanks for each physical characteristic such as your eye color...bone structure ... nerves ... organs ... muscles ... your height ...size ...shape...hair...senses...health...all of you! Smile and give thanks that you are a beautiful image of God. Draw your hands or feet, and inside the drawing list words, images, or phrases describing your body as holy. Or find a photo of yourself, attach it to a blank page in your journal, and, near the photo, list the ways you have used your body to serve others.

4. Compose a "body prayer" celebrating your journey toward wholeness and holiness (e.g., singing, dancing, moving to music, skipping, laughing, leaping, jumping, walking, sitting, lying down).

5. Be aware of any new insights, images, feelings, or thoughts that emerge during your "body prayer." Record these experiences in your prayer journal.

6. Ask God to reveal to you anything you need to do or change in your life in order to foster a greater harmony and unity between your body, mind, and spirit such as fasting, exercising, studying, resting, eating balanced meals, praying, or relaxing. Listen to God's response.

7. Pray for the courage and strength you need to adopt a more balanced and wholistic approach to your life. Decide on a plan of action for your spiritual journey. Begin by deciding on one thing you will do today to become a more holy and whole person.

Desert Mother Syncletica

(Fifth Century)

Introduction

Amma (Mother) Syncletica was a desert monastic woman who lived in fifth-century Egypt. Since many of her sayings employ nautical images, scholars believed that Syncletica may have come from the seaport of Alexandria. The desert mothers are believed to have lived in the fifth century, at which time the eremitical life was developing into new, small ascetical communities. However, there were some women who lived alone in the desert before this time.

Amma Syncletica's sayings use images that are provocative and clear, emphasizing the importance of balance and stability in the spiritual life: "Just as one cannot build a ship unless one has nails, so it is impossible to be saved without humility"; "You were iron, but fire has the rust off you"; "If you find yourself in a monastery do not go to another place, for that will harm you a great deal. Just as the bird who abandons the eggs she was sitting on prevents them from hatching so the monk or the nun grows cold and their faith dies, when they go from one place to another."[1]

Reflection

Amma Syncletica said, "There are many who live in the mountains and behave as if they were in the town, and they are wasting their time. It is possible to be a solitary in one's mind while living in a crowd, and it is possible for one who is a solitary to live in the crowd of one's own thoughts."[2]

Discussion Starters

1. What role does solitude play in the spiritual journey?

2. Do you agree with Amma Syncletica's saying that "it is possible to be a solitary in one's mind while living in a crowd"? Why? Why not? Do you agree with Amma Syncletica's saying that "it is possible for one who is a solitary to live in the crowd of one's own thoughts"? Why? Why not?

3. How can solitude — making time and space for prayerful reflection — affect the choices you make in your daily life?

4. What can you do to integrate and balance solitude and activity in your life now?

Prayer Experience

1. Close your eyes. Breathe slowly and deeply. Allow the tension to flow out of each area of your body beginning at the top of your head and going all the way down to the bottom of your feet. After spending a few minutes in silence, journey to the still point of your being.

2. Open yourself to God's love. Allow this love to fill you with joy ... strength ... faith ... love ... peace ... energy ... enthusiasm ... compassion ... wisdom ... fortitude ... anything you need to be a radiant reflection of God's love to others. Now, observe God's light shining through you in a powerful new way.

3. Reflect on your need for solitude, making time and space for prayerful reflection in your spiritual life. Be aware of how you can integrate and balance solitude and activity in your life now. Make a plan or calendar and schedule quiet time — no matter how busy you seem to be. Some possibilities include getting up ten minutes earlier for quiet prayer; taking a walk with God at lunch; enjoying and relaxing in a long shower or bath in the late evening; closing your eyes and repeating a prayer word or phrase to center yourself on the way to or from work (except when driving). Decide on a plan you will try for

one or two weeks. Then, after this period of time, change and adjust your plan, if necessary, to meet your unique needs and experience.

4. Take a walk or look out a window. Be aware of God's presence in everything you see, touch, taste, smell, hear. Let the air caress your body. Experience the beauty of creation and humanity. Be aware of your oneness with all creatures and with God. Celebrate the gift of life in whatever way feels real and natural to you.

5. Compose your own mantra or prayer phrase to use during busy times of the day, such as when you are showering, dressing, putting on makeup, washing dishes, doing the laundry, gardening, driving the car, doing routine outdoor or household chores. Examples are "God, I delight in you"; "God fill me with your _____" (peace, patience, joy, strength, courage, goodness, wisdom, discernment).

6. Ask God to help you integrate and balance solitude and activity in your life now. Draw, create, or find a symbol reminding you of your need for interior renewal, relaxation, and quiet in your life. Place this symbol in a prominent place in your home or work site.

7. Reflect on God's grace acting powerfully in the events of your daily life. Get in touch with God's presence in every event, activity, and relationship of your day. As you do so, be aware of any feelings that emerge: joy, peace, anxiety, worry, happiness, stress. Record these feelings and any fresh insights into God's presence in your life in your prayer journal.

Paula

(347–404)

Introduction

Paula was born into an old Roman aristocratic family on May 5, 347. Her mother, Blaesilla, was descended from the Scipio and Gracchi families. Her father, Rogatus, was said to be a descendant of Agamemnon. Paula married Toxotius, a relative of the renowned noble family Aeneas and Julii. Jerome, in the *Life of Paula*, 3, described Paula's marriage, children, and widowhood:

> Thus nobly born, Paula through her fruitfulness and her chastity won approval from all, from her husband first, then from her relatives, and lastly from the whole city. She bore five children; Blaesilla, for whose death I consoled her while at Rome; Paulina, who has left the reverend and admirable Pammachius to inherit both her vows and property, to whom also I addressed a little book on her death; Eustochium, who is now in the holy places, a precious necklace of virginity and of the church; Rufina, whose untimely end overcame the affectionate heart of her mother; and Toxotius, after whom she had no more children.[1]

According to Jerome's memories of her life, when Toxotius died, Paula's grief over her husband's death was so deep that she nearly died herself. Then, as soon as her mourning ended, she chose to dedicate her life fully to the service of God.

Paula, one of the richest women of her day, was known for her simplicity, poverty, and humility. She gave all her earthly goods to the poor and, according to Jerome's account of her life, died leaving nothing behind but a debt, which "Eustochium still owes and indeed cannot hope to pay off by her own exertions; only the mercy of Christ can free her from it."[2]

A close companion to Jerome for twenty years, Paula shared his devotion to the Scriptures, often challenging him with questions and providing insights into the meaning of different verses. Recalling Paula's intelligence and clarity, Jerome recalled, "Whenever I stuck fast and honestly confessed myself at fault, she would by no means rest content but would force me by fresh questions to point out to her which of many different solutions seemed to me the most probable." After mastering the Hebrew language, Paula would chant the psalms in Hebrew without a hint of Latin pronunciation.[3]

Jerome tells us that Paula loved her family dearly: "I must not pass over in silence the joy which Paula felt when she heard her little granddaughter and namesake, the child of Laeta and Toxotius, in her cradle sing 'alleluia' and falter out the words 'grandmother' and 'aunt.' Likewise, Paula and her daughter shared a very close relationship. Jerome describes Eustochium's compassionate care of her mother when Paula was ill: "She sat by Paula's bedside, she fanned her, she supported her head, she arranged her pillows, she chafed her feet, she rubbed her stomach, she smoothed down the bedclothes, she heated hot water, she brought towels."[4]

Jerome's words reveal the intense grief he felt when his dear friend Paula died on January 26, 404: "Who could tell the tale of Paula's dying with dry eyes? She fell into a most serious illness and thus gained what she most desired, power to leave us and to be joined more fully to the Lord. . . . If we mourn, it is for ourselves and not for her; yet even so, if we persist in weeping for one who reigns with Christ, we shall seem to envy her her glory."[5]

Reflection

Paula's intelligence showed her that her death was near. Her body and limbs grew cold and only in her holy breast did the warm beat of the living soul continue. Yet, as though she were leaving strangers to go home to her own people, she whispered the verses of the psalmist, "Lord, I have loved the habitation of your house and the place where your honour dwells" (Ps. 26:8), and "How amiable are your tabernacles,

O Lord of hosts! My soul longs and faints for the courts of the Lord"
(Ps. 84:2–3), and "I had rather be an outcast in the house of my God
than to dwell in the tents of wickedness" (Ps. 84:11). When I asked
her why she remained silent, refusing to answer my call, and whether
she was in pain, she replied in Greek that she had no suffering and
that all things were to her eyes calm and tranquil. After this she said
no more but closed her eyes and kept repeating the verses just quoted,
down to the moment in which she breathed out her soul, but in a tone
so low that we could scarcely hear what she said. Raising her finger
also to her mouth, she made the sign of the cross upon her lips. Then
her breath failed her and she gasped for death; yet even when her soul
was eager to break free, she turned the death-rattle (which comes at
last to all) into the praise of the Lord. The bishop of Jerusalem and
some from other cities were present, also a great number of the lower
clergy, both priests and levites. The entire monastery was filled with vir-
gins and monks. As soon as Paula heard the bridegroom saying, "Rise
up, my love, my fair one, my dove, and come away: for lo, the winter
is past, the rain is over and gone," she answered joyfully, "The flowers
appear on the earth; the time to cut them has come" (Song 2:10–12)
and "I believe that I shall see the good things of the Lord in the land of
the living" (Ps. 27:13).[6]

Discussion Starters

1. What can you learn about mutuality and partnership in relationships from Jerome's account of his friendship with Paula?

2. What is the significance of relationships in your faith journey?

3. What do you need to let go of now to prepare for your death
   and passage into the fullness of God's love?

4. How can trust in God's love enable us to overcome our fears
   of death and help us to live life more fully and freely now?

Prayer Experience

1. Be attentive to your breathing. As you inhale, breathe in
   God's overwhelming love for you. As you exhale, breathe out

God's boundless love for others. Do this for several minutes until you are relaxed.

2. Imagine that you are present at your own death. Be aware of the place ... the time ... the presence of others ... the pain or lack of pain ... people with whom you want to share some special messages such as ... "thank you" ... "please forgive me" ... "I love you" ... "I forgive you" ... "I will miss you" ... "I will pray for you" ... "goodbye." Be attentive to your conversation with others ... with God ... your feelings ... thoughts ... images ... insights ... hopes ... dreams ... as you prepare for the final letting go. When the moment of your death finally comes ... you journey toward a bright light ... you see God walking toward you. God embraces you tenderly ... smiles at you ... looks at you with profound love and welcomes you to heaven. Listen to God share with you some special words of praise and thanks ... delight in being in the presence of the Holy One whom you have longed to see face to face for so long. ... Pray for family members ... friends ... relatives ... people who will miss you or who may need special help. Be aware of any family members ... friends ... acquaintances ... saints ... angels ... Mary, our heavenly mother ... whom you encounter in heaven. You may wish to have a conversation with one or more of them.

3. Reflect on your life now. Ask God to reveal to you ways that you can prepare yourself for your death by letting go of fear and experiencing the freedom of the children of God. Be aware that death has no power over you. From the beginning of your existence God has loved you. You have been embraced by love every day of your life. When you die God will embrace you with the fullness of love. Pray this passage with the apostle Paul: "For I am convinced that neither death, nor life, nor angels, nor rulers, nor things present, nor things to come, nor powers, nor height, nor depth, nor anything else in all creation will be able to separate us from the love of God in Christ Jesus our Lord" (Rom. 8:38, NRSV).

4. Compose a prayer, song, poem, or dance of praise or draw a symbol or mandala (a drawing that can be made from a variety of shapes and whose edges of the boundary are equidistant from the center point) of thanksgiving for the wonderful ways God has loved you throughout your life. Get in touch with some of these events by drawing a timeline from your birth to now listing the major milestones and relationships that have occurred (e.g., birth/baptism, early childhood 1–5, primary school 6–9, intermediate 10–13, teen 14–18, young adult 19–21, marriage, and so on). Share your "prayerful expression" of thanksgiving with significant others such as family, friends, a spiritual director, a prayer/faith sharing group, and others.

5. Select a mantra or short prayer verse such as "Lord Jesus, free and save me from this _____ (fear, anxiety, sadness, compulsion)," or "Jesus, fill me with your courage _____ (when I worry, lose hope, face this temptation)," or create your own to remind you that God's saving power is always with you, setting you free from all your fears. Repeat it throughout the day and night especially in times when you experience sadness, anxiety, worry, compulsions, fear, temptation, oppression, or pain.

6. Offer thanks for the gifts God has given you. Ask yourself these questions:

   • "What gifts has God given me?"

   • "How I have used these special gifts in loving service to others?"

   • "If I were to die today, what spiritual riches would I leave behind?"

   • "How have I experienced God's deep love through family? friends? faith community? church? the sacraments? life? other people? the earth? the world?"

   • "How can I live and celebrate life more fully now?"

7. Record your responses to these questions in your prayer journal and/or share your responses to these questions with significant others in your life. Offer thanks for your close friends and partners in your faith journey.

Dhuoda

(b. 803)

Introduction

Dhuoda was born in 803 into a noble family in the Frankish kingdom. She married Bernhard of Septimania, a relative of the Carolingian kings, in the palace at Aachen on June 29, 824. Dhuoda gave birth to her first son, William, on November 29, 826, and to a second son on March 22, 841. In the summer of 841, Bernhard, motivated by political ambitions and jealousy, gave up their son William as a hostage to Charles the Bald and took their second son away before baptism to be educated under his influence. Dhuoda lived under house arrest in a castle in France because Bernhard decided that this fostered his political purposes. In response to this forced separation from her children, Dhuoda wrote her *Manual* between November 30, 841, and February 2, 843. It was addressed to her son William, telling him how to live a virtuous life and how to attain eternal life. Dhuoda's *Manual*, not unlike a catechism, covered the basics of the Christian faith such as worship of God, the Trinity, the theological virtues of faith, hope, and charity, advice on how to pray, prayers to recite, respect for religious and secular authority, the practice of the eight beatitudes, and the seven gifts of the Holy Spirit. She advised William to be patient and to give alms to the poor. Because Dhuoda passed on her beliefs and religious values in this *Manual* to her children, some scholars refer to her as "the Frankish mother."[1]

As a female writer and a learned lay woman in the Carolingian age, when education among the laity was a rarity, Dhuoda not only provides unique insights into the spiritual and cultural interests of her age, but also reveals the inner journey of an out-

standing woman and a courageous mother. As one author puts
it, "From Dhuoda we learn how a private person viewed the
Carolingian world."[2]

The epitaph of Dhuoda reflects the esteem of the people of her
era for this remarkable woman and the popular early tradition of
addressing God in prayer with a variety of names:

> Dhuoda's body, formed of earth
> Lies buried in this tomb.
>> Immense King receive her!
> Here the earth has received in its bowels
> The all too fragile clay which belonged to it.
>> Benign King, grant her pardon!
> Under and over her are the opaque depths
> Of the grave, bathed in her wounds.
>> O King, forgive her sins!
> O you of all ages and sexes who come
> And go here, I beg you, say this:
>> Great Hagios, unlock her chains!
>
> ...Clement God, come to her aid!
> No one should leave her without having read.
> I urge all that they may pray, saying this:
>> Almus, give her rest!
> And command, Benign One, that she be given
>> Eternal light with the saints in the end.
> And may she receive Amen after her death![3]

Dhuoda's Manual

Here Begins the Manual of Dhuoda, which she sent to her son, William:

Having noticed that most women in this world are able to live
and enjoy their children, but seeing myself, Dhuoda, living far
away from you, my dear son William, filled with anxiety because
of this, and with the desire to be of aid to you, I am sending you
this little manual, written by me, for your scrutiny and education,
rejoicing in the fact that, though I am absent in body, this little

book will recall to your mind, as you read it, the things you are required to do for my sake.[4]

Reflection

Prayer is called oratio, "prayer," sort of oris ratio, reason of the mouth. But I, Dhuoda, lukewarm and lazy, weak and always tending toward that which is low, neither a long nor a short prayer pleases me. . . . Say, not only in the church, but wherever the opportunity presents itself, pray and say, "Mercy-giving and Merciful, Just and Pious, Clement and True, have pity on Your creation, whom You created and redeemed with Your blood; have pity on me, and grant that I may walk in Your paths and Your justice; give me memory and sense that I may understand, believe, love, fear, praise, and thank You and be perfect in every good work through proper faith and good will, O Lord, my God. Amen."[5]

Discussion Starters

1. From the passages above, what characteristics do you think Dhuoda possessed?

2. What insights does Dhuoda reveal about the process of faith-sharing that can be helpful for us today?

3. What role do parents play in their children's faith formation? How can parents, grandparents, aunts, uncles, cousins, relatives, the extended family share their faith stories with the younger generation and with each other?

4. What can you do to nurture the spiritual development of your spouse? children? family? friends? faith community?

Prayer Experiences

1. Close your eyes and call to mind an image of a loving mother. Imagine yourself as a strong, wise, playful, courageous, compassionate, caring mother. See your child or children. Observe what you do to show your love and concern for them each

day. (If you have children or grandchildren you may wish to imagine yourself caring for them in this meditation.)

2. Be aware of any thoughts, feelings, sensations, insights, or images that emerge when you reflect on yourself as mother.

3. Reflect on the sources of stress and frustration in your relationship with your children. Be aware of any failures or hurts for which you need forgiveness, healing, and transformation in your relationships with them. You may wish to list them on paper.

4. When you have finished, ask God to forgive and heal you. Then imagine God transforming your relationship with your children and filling you with whatever you need to nurture them more effectively. Then ask your children for forgiveness for anything you have done to hurt or offend them. Offer forgiveness for their failures. Do something special with your children to celebrate your mutual forgiveness and love.

5. Now imagine God embracing, loving, nurturing your children. Observe what God does to meet your children's needs. Be aware that God loves your children infinitely more than you do and holds them close to the Divine Heart. Surrender your children, one by one, to God's loving care. To symbolize your letting go, open your hands, palms up. Imagine your children, as they are. Say their names and a prayer of your choice or something like this: "_____, I let go of all anxiety about you now. I see you as you are and always will be, loved tenderly and completely by God"; "_____, I let go of my need to control your life. I set you free to be who you are called to be as God's beautiful image in this world."

6. Write a letter or record a tape or video for your children about your faith journey. Share with them some important milestones and relationships in your faith journey. Include the story of their grandparents, extended family, and previous generations. You could use photo albums, music, movies, or videos to share the good news of your "family gospel" with your children. This suggestion may take time to complete and

you may wish to plan a special family celebration to proclaim
your "family's gospel" with extended family, friends, neighbors,
faith community, or others.

7. With song, dance, poetry, or some other form of art, compose
a prayer of thanks for the beauty and goodness of your children. Or you may wish to compose a prayer expressing your
hopes and dreams for your children's spiritual growth.

Hildegard of Bingen

(1098–1179)

Introduction

The youngest of ten children, Hildegard was born in 1098 at Bickelheim (in modern Germany). At the age of eight she was placed by her family under the care of Jutta, an anchoress at Disibodenberg, to be educated in the Benedictine way of life. When she was eighteen, Hildegard became a Benedictine nun. After Jutta's death in 1136, the nuns elected Hildegard as abbess. Several years later, Hildegard became aware of a prophetic call and committed herself to a public and literary career. During the next forty years, she authored three theological treatises, a medical and a scientific encyclopedia, mystical treatises, poetry, music, including a liturgical song cycle, and the first European morality play. In addition, before her death at the age of eighty-one, Hildegard founded two monasteries, undertook several major preaching tours, counseled numerous pilgrims and visitors, and kept an extensive correspondence. As a writer, preacher, prophet, mystic, and visionary, Hildegard corresponded with church and political leaders of her time (Bernard of Clairvaux, Thomas Becket, and popes, such as Eugene III, Anastasius IV, Adrian IV, and Alexander III).[1]

Hildegard traveled and preached in cathedrals, warning the bishops and people about the corruption and abuses in the church. "Her ceaseless complaints about a society run and ruled by men, seemed to reflect a profound disillusionment with a social order which gave women few rights and no power."[2] Hildegard regarded her gender as an integral dimension of her prophetic call because she felt strongly that she lived in such an effeminate age that God had to call women to do men's work.[3]

Hildegard received twenty-six visions on such topics as the love of God for humanity in creation, salvation, and the church, and wrote them down in her first prophetic book, *Scivias*. Aware of her prophetic call, Hildegard opened this book with this warning to the visionary: "Let those who see the inner meaning of Scripture, yet do not wish to proclaim or preach it, take instruction, for they are lukewarm and sluggish in persevering the justice of God."[4] Often she complained about the lack of zeal in male prelates and teachers: "Nowadays the Catholic faith wavers and the Gospel limps among the peoples ... and the food of life — the divine Scripture — has grown tepid." God instructs her to proclaim the Word, even though she is "trampled underfoot by men 'because of Eve's transgression.' "[5]

Archbishop Henry of Mainz declared her spiritual writings as authentic. In 1979, Pope John Paul II, on the eight hundredth anniversary of Hildegard's death, called her an "outstanding saint, a light to her people and her time [who] shines out more brightly today."[6]

Reflection

God is Life.

All living creatures are, so to speak, sparks from the radiation of God's brilliance, and these sparks emerge from God like the rays of the sun.

How would God be known as life if not through the fact that the realm of the living, which glorifies and praises God, also emerges from God? On this account God has established the living, burning sparks as a sign of the brilliance of the divine renown.

But if God did not give off these sparks, how would the divine flame become fully visible? And how would God be known as the Eternal One if no brilliance emerged from God? For no creature exists that lacks a radiance — be it greenness or seed, buds or beauty. Otherwise it would not be a creature at all.[7]

Discussion Starters

1. "The fiery firmament is a footstool to the throne of God," observes Matthew Fox in his commentary on Hildegard of Bingen, and "all creatures are sparks from this fire. We sparks come from God."[8] What thoughts, insights, feelings, or images does Hildegard's vision of God's relationship to the cosmos stir within you?

2. How can the creatures of the earth draw us into adoration?

3. In what ways are you a steward of creation? How can you show a gentle respect for the earth and all creatures?

4. Most earth-related spiritualities focus on the interdependence between creatures and human beings. What can you do to join with others to save the earth's resources and live in harmony with all creatures in our earth community?

Prayer Experience

1. Relax in a quiet place and focus on God's loving presence within you, above you, below you, around you, everywhere.

2. Look at your surroundings and the people you love. Be aware that God is present loving you and loving through you in those surroundings and people. Rejoice and offer thanks for specific people and places where you have experienced giving and receiving love.

3. Go outdoors or imagine that you are outdoors. Look at and listen to the sounds of nature. Breathe deeply. Allow the beauty of the earth to fill you and draw you into adoration.

4. Cultivate a gentle respect for the earth by smelling flowers, petting animals, feeding birds, hugging trees, cultivating the earth, planting a garden, lying on the grass, breathing deeply, walking in the rain, etc. As you touch nature, reflect on what God is teaching you about the earth and your interdependence with other creatures.

5. Reflect on ways you can heal, nurture, and renew the earth by being a better earth steward and caretaker of creation. Compose a prayer, song, poem, psalm, or dance of healing for the earth.

6. Realize that the earth is our teacher. Be open to any new learnings that mother earth wants to share with you. Ask God to reveal to you ways you can deal with eco-issues in a meaningful, concrete way, e.g., simplify your lifestyle by becoming more self-sustaining in food, fuel, water.

7. Decide on one practical way that you will work together with others to effect change in society and public policy for global environmental stewardship. Organizations such as North American Coalition on Region and Ecology (NACRE, 5 Thomas Circle N.W., Washington, DC 20005) have numerous activities that you can participate in depending on your interest.

Beatrice of Nazareth

(1200-1268)

Introduction

Not much is known about Beatrice of Nazareth's early life. Her father was Barthelmy de Vleeschouwer. Her mother used the psalter to teach Beatrice to read in Latin at age seven. Unfortunately, she died when Beatrice was seven. At eight or nine she was placed in the care of the Beguines at Leau (Zoutleeuw) in Belgium. When she was fifteen Beatrice entered the Cistercian order, and one year later she professed her vows on Pentecost 1216. Her father, her brother, and several of her sisters also became Cistercians and may have professed vows with her in 1216. At LaRamee Beatrice learned manuscript copying and developed an important spiritual friendship with Ida of Nivelles. Beatrice lived in three Cistercian houses that her father had founded, at Florival, Val-des-Vierges, and Nazareth. She was abbess of Nazareth for thirty years; she died there on August 29, 1268.

Beatrice dictated *The Seven Steps of Love* to her confessor, who translated it into Latin. The steps are as follows: (1) The desire to serve God has its origins in love; one reflects on one's motives and desires to love more deeply. (2) One strives to serve God out of love alone, seeking only to please God. (3) At this stage one struggles because of an inability to love God completely. (4) One is filled with such overwhelming love for God that one cannot always control one's body. (5) At this stage the more one experiences God's love, the more one wants this love. (6) One finds total freedom and deep love with God; one cannot be affected by evil. (7) In this, the highest level, one experiences a passionate desire for Christ. In spite of the difficulties and trials of life, one is confident that in the end God's love will prevail.[1]

The following passage describes Beatrice's vision of the power of God's love.

Reflection

Sometimes it happens that love is sweetly awakened in the soul and joyfully arises and moves in the heart of itself without us doing anything at all. And then the heart is so powerfully touched by love, so keenly drawn into love and so strongly seized by love and so utterly mastered by love and so tenderly embraced by love that it entirely yields itself to love. And in this it experiences a great proximity to God, a spiritual radiance, a marvelous bliss, a noble freedom, an ecstatic sweetness, a great overpowering by the strength of love, and an overflowing abundance of immense delight.

And then she feels that all her senses are sanctified by love and her will has become love, and that she is so deeply immersed and so engulfed in the abyss of love that she herself has turned entirely into love. Then the beauty of love has bedecked her, . . . the nobility of love has enveloped her, the purity of love has adorned her, and the sublimity of love has drawn her upwards and so united herself with her that she always must be love and do nothing but the deeds of love.[2]

Discussion Starters

1. As you reflect upon Beatrice of Nazareth's reflection, what new insights come to you about God's love for you?

2. What does it mean to gently accept yourself? your body? emotions? personality? gifts and abilities?

3. Do you experience God's unconditional acceptance of yourself as you are right now?

4. In what area do you feel you most need to be loved by God now?

Prayer Experience

1. Use some classical or instrumental music to help you to relax. Close your eyes. Allow the music to soothe you like ocean waves dancing on the seashore.

2. Begin your prayer by gently accepting yourself as you are right now — in your physical, spiritual, and psychological growth.

3. Affirm all parts of your body, your emotions, your personality, your gifts and skills. Feel yourself — your entire being — accepted by and loved totally and completely by God. Open yourself to the boundless, passionate, tender love of God for you as you are right now.

4. Be aware that you are in a constant loving communion with God, who dwells within the depths of your being. Spend time in silence, simply being in love with God.

5. Listen as God speaks words of acceptance and affirmation to you such as:

   "I love you."

   "You are mine."

   "Your body is my special dwelling place."

   "I will forgive your failures and heal your wounds."

   "I will love you forever with all my love."

   "I have given you special gifts: _____ [name these gifts and abilities]."

   "You are a vibrant reflection of my love."

6. Be open to whatever God wishes to do to lead you to a deeper intimacy with God and a greater acceptance of yourself.

7. In a prayerful conversation with God, share any insights, feelings, or thoughts that emerge. Record any important insights from this conversation in your prayer journal. Do something special to celebrate your self-acceptance. (Example: Sing, dance, laugh, be yourself! Share your inner riches with a friend over dinner.)

Hadewijch of Brabant

(Thirteenth Century)

Introduction

Little biographical information is available on Hadewijch other than what is found in her writings. Often referred to as "the Brabant Mystic" because the dialect in which she wrote is that spoken in Brabant, scholars tell us that she lived in the first quarter of the thirteenth century and that her letters and poems were probably written between 1220 and 1240. Her writings reflect a knowledge of Latin, French, numerology, astronomy, music, and the rules of rhetoric. She demonstrated a familiarity with the love poetry of her time. Hadewijch wrote thirty-one letters, forty-five stanzaic poems, fourteen visions, and twenty-nine poems.

Hadewijch may have lived in Antwerp or in Brussels, where her work was popular in the fourteenth century at the abbey of Groenendaal. Her letters indicate that she may have been a nun or have lived in a small community of religious women. Some scholars believe that she either founded or belonged to a Beguine group and had become a spiritual director for a number of young Beguines. It is the opinion of these experts that Hadewijch was ousted from her Beguine community and that she may have become homeless and spent her final days nursing the sick and suffering.[1] However, there is no proof of this, and modern research portrays Hadewijch as a noble woman who lived like a recluse.

In her letters and poems Hadewijch appears as an intelligent, educated, compassionate woman who advocated service to the poor and wrote passionately about mystical love. Her writings are an example of early *minnemystiek*, a form of mysticism in which courtly love poetry is applied to mystic experience. "In Hadewijch scholarship, *minne* has often been identified with God or Christ, which classified her thinking as yet another example of Christ or bridal mysticism," observed scholar Ria Vanderauwera. "Yet she does not often refer to Christ, to his birth or suffering, nor does she make great use of the bridal theme." N. de Paepe, after extensive research on Hadewijch, concluded that in Hadewijch's writings, *minne* "is not God, not Christ, not even...the love of God for humanity but the love of a human being for God."[2]

The following passage from Hadewijch's letters contains images of courtly love to describe our human love for God:

> Love's burning desire is a precious gift; the lover knows this and asks no more. For this is love's truth: she joins two in one being, makes sweet sour, strangers neighbors, and the lowly noble. She makes the healthy sick and the sick healthy; she cripples those who are sound of limb and heals the wounded. To the ignorant she reveals the wide roads they must wander in weariness and teaches them all that shall be learned in the school of highest love.[3]

Reflection

Later, on Easter Sunday, I had gone to God.... And from the total Being of that Countenance received all understanding, and thus I read all my judgments. A voice that issued from this Countenance resounded so fearfully that it made itself heard above everything. And it said to me: "Behold, ancient one, you have called me and sought me, what and who I, Love, am.... See and receive my Spirit! With regard to all things, know what I, Love, am in them! And when you fully bring me yourself, as pure humanity in myself, through all the ways of perfect Love, you shall have fruition of me as the Love who I am. And then you will be love, as I am Love. And you shall not live less than what I, Love, am, from that day until the death that will make you alive.... Go forth, and live what I am; and return bringing me full divinity, and have fruition of me as who I am."

Then I returned to myself, and I understood all I have just said; and I remained to gaze fixedly upon my delightful sweet Love.[4]

Discussion Starters

1. How has prayer and meditation helped you to experience God's presence in your life?

2. What is God revealing to you about Divine Love in this passage from Hadewijch?

3. What impact does your experience of God's love for you have on your relationship with others?

4. What impact does your experience of human love have on your relationship with God?

Prayer Experience

1. Sit in a comfortable position. Close your eyes. Begin to relax your body. Begin with your head, face, and neck....Release any tightness in these areas....Relax your shoulders, arms, hands....Release any tightness in your stomach, back, hips, legs, and feet... etc.

2. Read slowly Hadewijch's meditation as if it was your mystical experience.

3. Become aware of God's presence. Let God hold you gently. Allow yourself to delight in God's tender embrace. "And then you will be Love as I am Love."

4. Be conscious of any new images or insights into your relationship with God.

5. Open yourself to the depth of God's beauty, glory, goodness, and passion revealed in your experience of human love.

6. Reflect on ways you have given love to others and received love from others. Offer thanks for these experiences.

7. Express your insights, feelings, thoughts, images, memories, and sensations of God's love and human love in your life in some creative way such as art, poetry, dance, drama, clay, song, or journaling.

Mechtild of Magdeburg

(1209–1282)

Introduction

Mechtild of Magdeburg was born in 1209 in a small town on the Elbe River in Germany, apparently of wealthy parents. As a child she experienced God's presence in vivid ways. She describes herself as God's "Playmate" (4:3).[1] "Your childhood was a companion of my Holy Spirit" (7:3). She participated in divine play: "God alone will play with [her] in a game of which the body knows nothing" (1:2). God leads "the child in you in wonderful ways" (1:25). The Holy Spirit filled her so fully that Mechtild believed she could not commit serious sin (4:2).

In 1210 Mechtild went to the city of Magdeburg and joined the Beguines, a group of women who lived in community, did not marry, and did not become nuns, but lived in the world and worked for a living. She quickly attracted a group of followers and friends. Mechtild spoke out against the abuses of clerics and the injustices present in church and society. As a result, she encountered ridicule, opposition, and questions about her orthodoxy.

When her health deteriorated, she left Magdeburg and was welcomed into the convent of Helfta, the home of Sts. Mechtild of Hackeborn and Gertrude the Great. There she found companionship and remained until her death in 1282.

Mechtild imaged God as a loving mother who "lifts her loved child from the ground to her knee" (4:22). She finds her soul in the Trinity, which is like "a mother's cloak wherein the child finds a home and lays its head on the maternal breast" (6:7).

In Mechtild's spirituality there is a profound unity of compassion and social action: "When we on earth pour out compassion

and mercy from the depths of our hearts and give to the poor
and dedicate our bodies to the service of the broken, to that very
extent do we resemble the Holy Spirit who is a compassionate
outpouring of the Creator and the Son" (6:32).

Reflection

Divine love is immensely great!
Great is its overflow,
   for Divine love is never still.
Always ceaselessly and tirelessly
   it pours itself out
   so that the small vessel which is ourselves
   might be filled to the brim
and might also overflow.

God speaks:
When your Easter comes
I shall be all around you,
I shall be through and through you
And I shall steal your body
And give you to your Love.[2]

Discussion Starters

1. As you look around you in the world, where do you see
   God's love?

2. As you reflect on your own suffering and the suffering of
   others, where do you see God being revealed?

3. What difference does the resurrection of Jesus make in your
   attitude toward suffering and death?

4. As you reflect on your own death, what changes do you want
   to make in your life?

Prayer Experience

1. Breathe slowly several times; become aware of each breath as you inhale and exhale. Feel it flowing through your body. Continue this until you feel relaxed.

2. Read Mechtild's words slowly and thoughtfully. Let her rich images and poetic language speak to your inner being.

3. During this time of reflection, ask God to reveal to you how much you are loved.

4. Be aware of times when you experienced suffering in your life. Choose one of these experiences to reflect on in depth.

5. Imagine the people, places, and circumstances that were present during this time of pain. Write down the positive and negative aspects of this suffering up to the present. Be aware of your feelings.

6. Picture Jesus close to you during this time of suffering. Jesus wants to heal and transform the pain of your past. Open yourself to the healing power of Jesus. Imagine Jesus looking at you with infinite compassion and loving you with immense love. Share your feelings with Jesus. Listen to Jesus' response.

7. Imagine tomorrow is your last day on earth. Make a list of things that you want to do today. Dialogue with Jesus about your fears, hopes, dreams, and anxieties about your death. When you finish the dialogue, read it back to yourself and be aware of any changes you want to make in your life now.

Mechtild of Hackeborn

(1241–1298)

Introduction

In 1248, at seven years old, Mechtild was brought by her mother to the monastery of Helfta to visit her older sister, Gertrude. Mechtild pleaded with her mother to be allowed to stay with the nuns. Her mother agreed, and Mechtild was educated at Helfta. At seventeen, Mechtild was received into this renowned community.

Because Mechtild had a beautiful singing voice, she became choir director and teacher. One of her students was Gertrude, later referred to as "the Great," who had begun studies at the abbey when she was five years old. Mechtild of Magdeburg, the former Beguine, came to Helfta as an older nun seeking refuge after she had alienated local church officials by her criticism of their abuses. These three women mystics of the thirteenth century, Gertrude the Great, Mechtild of Magdeburg, and Mechtild of Hackeborn, were friends and companions on the spiritual journey in their home at Helfta.

The liturgy was central to Mechtild's spirituality. She told her students "that any deed performed for the worship of God, however small it might be, resounds everlastingly as a soft melody from the heart of the person to the heart of God."[1]

In addition to performing her choral duties and teaching, Mechtild participated in the everyday chores of the monastery: spinning, dyeing, sewing, and cooking. She ministered to the sisters who were sick and dying. Comforting a sister who was dying, Mechtild reassured her: "What shipman would cast his goods willfully into the sea when he is coming to the harbor in peace? No shipman would do so, no more will I with her. But I shall take her soul joyfully to myself and not cast it from me."[2]

The sisters considered Mechtild as their special intercessor with God in times of great crisis. In 1294, when the monastery was threatened by the soldiers of the Emperor Adolph of Nassau, Mechtild prayed that the community be spared from harm. "You will not see a single soldier," she assured her sisters. The monastery experienced the divine protection she promised.[3]

Mechtild constantly prayed that God would bestow abundant blessing on her sisters and help them grow in virtues and good works.

To those who sought her advice, Mechtild offered affirmation and direction. As she prayed compassionately for a woman overburdened with physical work, Mechtild imaged the woman kneeling before Christ while Christ poured a healing balm on her hands. To a sister who was suffering from depression, Mechtild shared this message from Christ: "Why is she troubled? I have given myself to her for the fulfillment of all her desires. I am her father by creation, her mother by redemption, her brother in the sharing of my kingdom, her sister by sweet companionship."[4]

An advocate of frequent reception of communion, Mechtild encouraged the nuns, especially those who struggled with scrupulosity, to draw close to Christ in the Eucharist. Mechtild challenged them to pray often for the needs of others. "One should be as liberal as a queen at the king's table."[5] Mechtild had deep trust in Christ's mercy and availability. "He is more easily possessed than a bit of thread or straw. A single wish, a sigh, is sufficient."[6]

Believing that God's infinite love is beyond all comprehension, Mechtild discovered deep peace. Even her limitations and weaknesses reminded her of God's goodness and her dependence on divine mercy. She shared her reflections with Gertrude: "In the light of eternal truth I now see clearly that all my love for those who were dear to me in this life is no more than a drop in the ocean in comparison with the love of the Sacred Heart for them. I see also why God permits persons to keep certain faults that humiliate and discipline them on the way of salvation."[7]

Mechtild died in 1298 at age fifty-seven after a three-year ill-ness. Sr. Jeremy Finnegan portrays Mechtild: "No one was more companionable, less singular."[8]

Reflection

If any obstacle arises in our service of God, whether from the attitude of others, from external circumstances, from our own desires or mem-ories, or from any other cause — whatever the impediment, we should take it as a messenger from God, sending it back . . . , so to speak, with praise and thanksgiving.[9]

When it is time to eat or to sleep, say in your heart: "Lord, in union with the love with which you created this useful thing for me, and your-self made use of it when you were on earth. I take it for your eternal praise and for my bodily need."[10]

We should be lovingly grateful not only for the spiritual blessings God gives us, but for all bodily necessities such as food and clothing, receiving them with a sincerely thankful heart and considering ourselves unworthy of them.[11]

Discussion Starters

1. How would your life change if you were to perceive obsta-cles and difficulties as "messengers from God," blessings in disguise?

2. How can you become a "prayer of praise and thanksgiving" to God?

3. In what ways can you show gratitude for life's daily miracles and blessings?

4. In what ways can you show appreciation to special people in your life?

Prayer Experience

1. Sit quietly in a comfortable chair or lie down on a rug or the bed. Close your eyes. Breathe deeply for several minutes. Be-

come aware of God's presence dwelling in your whole being. Allow yourself to sink slowly and deeply into this everlasting love and see it filling your mind, body, will, and emotions.

2. Use a prayer phrase or a mantra to center yourself in thanks and praise for God's rich blessings in your daily life (examples: "Praise God," "Thank you, Jesus," "Yes," "Alleluia").

3. As you journey to the depths of your being, do not focus on images, thoughts, feelings, or anything else. Simply relax and be a prayer of praise and thanksgiving to God.

4. Become aware of obstacles or difficulties that cause you frustration or anxiety (examples: physical illness, stress at work or at home, difficult relationships, family problems, loss of a loved one, unemployment, financial pressures). Imagine these obstacles as "special messengers" from God to you. Invite these "special messengers" to reveal God's direction and provident care in your life. Then offer thanks for these "special messengers" and let them go, one by one. Be aware of any new insights that you discover about God's blessings and record these in your prayer journal.

5. Take a walk in a park, go for a moonlit swim, enjoy a rooftop view of the stars. Be still and observe the natural beauty of a sunrise, a sunset, snow falling, leaves changing, flowers blossoming, and other little miracles. Touch, taste, smell, breathe, and feel the beauty of creation around you. Let this be your prayer of praise to God.

6. Meditate for half an hour in the bathtub. Put a "Do Not Disturb" sign on the door. Light a scented candle. Turn the lights out. Slide neck deep into the warm water and just be with God in thanksgiving.

7. Recall wonderful qualities or deeds that you treasure in one of your family members or close friends. With song, dance, poetry, or some form of art, compose a prayer of appreciation for these gifts. Share, if possible, your prayer of gratitude with this person.

Gertrude the Great

(1256–1302)

Introduction

At the age of five Gertrude was placed in the care of the nuns of Helfta in Germany. There she was educated in the theological sciences, learned to copy manuscripts, and eventually became a Benedictine nun. She was a friend and student of Mechtild of Magdeburg, who also resided at Helfta.

Gertrude's mystical visions began when she was twenty-five. Gertrude describes her powerful conversion experience: "I was twenty-five years old, and it was the Monday (a Monday most fraught with salvation for me) before the feast of the Purification of Mary ... at the hour after Compline for which one longs, in the early hours of dusk." As she let go of her "preoccupation with the world and court," Jesus spoke to her in a vision: "You have sucked honey among thorns; return to me at last, and I shall make you drunk with the rushing river of my divine pleasure" (2.1).[1]

Gertrude's devotion to the Sacred Heart of Jesus reflects her insight that the heart of Jesus is the bridge between Jesus' divinity and his humanity. "As Gertrude once prostrated at the feet of our Lord Jesus, and kissed His Wounds ... she saw a stream breaking forth from the Heart of Jesus, which appeared to water all the place where she was. She understood that this stream was the efficacy of the prayers which she offered at His feet."[2]

In her *Revelations* Gertrude's visions emphasize the healing power of prayer. She teaches that no matter how great the suffering or pain we experience, praying with others will have a healing effect on us. Gertrude reminds us that when we are aware of our burdens we should ask others to pray for us.[3]

Reflection

As the Saint prayed for a person who had requested her prayers with great humility, both personally and through others, she saw our Lord approach this person, encompassing her with celestial light, and pouring forth on her in the midst of this splendor all the graces which she had hoped to receive through the merits of the prayers of Gertrude. Our Lord taught her by this that when anyone confides in the prayers of another, with a firm confidence that through their intercession they will receive grace from God, the Lord in His goodness pours forth His benedictions on them according to the measure of their desires and their faith, even when he to whose prayers they have recommended themselves neglects to pray for them.[4]

Discussion Starters

1. Can you remember a time when you prayed for others? What difference did your prayer make?

2. Can you remember a time when others prayed for you? If so, what difference did it make to you? If not, what difference do you think it could have made?

3. What people or groups would you identify as intercessory prayer groups? What have you learned from these people or groups about the power of intercessory prayer?

4. Who and what do you feel God is calling you to pray for at this time?

Prayer Experience

1. Take several deep breaths and let go of any tension in your body.

2. With your eyes closed and your body relaxed, get in touch with your spiritual journey from its beginning, i.e., from your birth onward. Reflect on the relationships, events, and circumstances of your life. Be aware of any times when you

experienced strength or comfort from the prayer support of others.

3. With your eyes open, write down descriptions of these occasions beginning with your birth and moving up to times in the present that you experienced the power of others' prayers in your life. Offer thanks for these experiences of grace.

4. Be aware of any blocks, fears, or anxieties that keep you from asking for the prayer support of others now.

5. Gently release those blocks into the loving heart of God, one by one, as you become aware of them. Imagine God opening your heart and filling it with trust and confidence that when you pray with others, God is also present.

6. As you let go and let God, become conscious of any feelings, images, thoughts, insights, memories, or sensations that occur. Record these experiences in your prayer journal.

7. Ask God to reveal to you any persons or situations for whom you could offer prayers. Be open also to sharing your needs for prayer with others. Invite others (family, friends, neighbors, community, church members) to join you in intercessory prayer for these needs. You may want to pursue the possibility of joining or starting a small faith community that prays daily for the needs of others and meets weekly, biweekly, or monthly for mutual prayer and support.

Clare of Assisi

(1194–1253)

Introduction

Clare was born in 1194 into the prosperous Offreduccio clan in Assisi in what is now Italy. Her father, Favarone, provided his family with a lovely large home near the cathedral of San Rufino. Before her birth a mysterious voice told her mother that Clare would be a bright light in the world. Clare was described as a prayerful, quiet, and obedient child.

Clare may have been in the Cathedral of San Rufino when Francis of Assisi preached there in 1210. By the time she was eighteen, Clare had met with him several times to receive spiritual direction. When Clare heard that her family had planned an arranged marriage for her, she sought Francis's advice.

On Palm Sunday, according to local custom, the daughters of the town's elite would line up before the bishop in their most beautiful gowns to receive their palms as the congregation watched. "On this particular Palm Sunday, Clare's turn came to go forward, but she did not rise.... Perhaps she slipped into a kind of rapture. It is public record, in any event, that the bishop saw her sitting with her family immobile, and walked down to hand her the palm himself." That same night Clare chose to withdraw from the world and leave her home.[1]

Clare, accompanied by a friend, walked to St. Mary's Church in Portiuncula, where Francis and his followers lived. There Francis cut off Clare's long hair and put on her the tunic that identified his small band of followers. Clare committed herself to a life of poverty and asceticism as a lover who runs to her Beloved "with swift pace, light step, unswerving feet, so that even your steps stir up no dust."[2]

After a brief stay in the Benedictine monastery of San Paolo delle Ancelle di Dio and Sant' Angelo di Panzo, Francis took Clare and her sister Catherine to San Damiano, one of the churches he had repaired. The sisters at San Damiano lived on alms and the work of their hands. They were enclosed in a house surrounded by a small garden.

Clare saw herself as a recipient of God's many gifts — gifts meant to be used for the good of others. Clare realized that the less she provided for herself the more she could trust in God's provident care. Clare associated contemplative prayer and evangelical poverty with economic poverty. In order to be receptive to God's love in prayer, one needs to let go of attachments to material possessions. In her prayer and poverty Clare felt that she had already experienced the kingdom of heaven through love: "You know, I am sure, that the kingdom of heaven is promised and given by the Lord only to the poor: for he who loves temporal things loses the fruit of love."[3]

We can perhaps comprehend the depths of Clare's commitment to evangelical poverty by reflecting on her hymn to poverty:

O blessed poverty
    who bestows eternal riches on those
    who love and embrace her
O holy poverty
    to those who possess and desire you
    God promises the kingdom of heaven
    and offers indeed eternal glory and blessed life!
O God-centered poverty
    whom the Lord Jesus Christ,
    Who ruled and now rules heaven and earth,
    Who spoke and things were made
    condescended to embrace before all else.[4]

In 1247 Clare began writing her own Rule because she could not accept the concept of ownership of property permitted in the Rule given her by Pope Innocent IV. On August 9, 1253, two days before her death, her Rule received papal approval. According to scholars, Clare is believed to be the first woman in the history of the church to write her own Rule. In chapter 8 of her Rule, Clare counsels her Sisters, the Poor Ladies (now known as Poor Clares), to live a life of poverty: "Nor should they be ashamed, for the Lord made himself poor for us in this world. This is that sublimity of the highest poverty which had made you, my dearest sisters, heirs and queens of the kingdom of heaven: poor in goods but exalted in virtue. May this be your portion which leads to the land of the living."[5]

Clare was canonized on August 12, 1255, two years after her death. She continues to inspire her followers today as a witness of God's marvelous deeds and as a mentor for contemporary women. "Clare, the new leader of women, was in every respect a most faithful daughter of the Church whom she served with all her strength and for the whole of her life."[6]

Reflection

Place your mind before the mirror of eternity!
Place your soul in the brilliance of glory!
Place your heart in the figure of the divine substance!
And transform your whole being into the image of the Godhead
    Itself through contemplation![7]

Discussion Starters

1. How can Clare of Assisi be a role model today for Christians who live in a materialistic society?

2. What connections would you make between contemplative prayer and simplicity of life?

3. Describe your experience of God's love in your life.

4. How are you called to image God in your relationships and in the ordinary events of daily life?

Prayer Experience

1. Find a comfortable relaxed position. Breathe deeply and slowly. Be aware of your body. Begin with your head and work through each muscle area in your body, alternately tensing and relaxing each area.

2. Read the reflection from Clare of Assisi slowly, as if Clare were speaking these words personally to you.

3. Be aware of any thoughts, feelings, insights, or images that come to mind.

4. In the stillness become aware that God dwells within you.

5. Imagine God loving you with overwhelming passion and immeasurable tenderness. See God permeating your entire being with infinite love. Open yourself to a new encounter with the transforming power of God. Experience God's unconditional love in the depths of your heart.

6. See yourself "acting as if" you are the image of God in your relationships. Observe the power of God flowing through you in the ordinary events of your daily life. Be aware of any images, insights, or feelings that emerge. Express these images, insights, or feelings in some creative way such as art, drama, dance, song, poetry, or clay.

7. Decide on one way you will be today the "hands and feet of God" to your family, friends, neighbors, co-workers, or others (examples: listen to a family member or friend who is upset or anxious and reflect back to him or her your acceptance and love; surprise your spouse or teenager by doing one of their chores; shop for an elderly neighbor; play an extra five minutes with a small child).

Angela of Foligno

(1248–1309)

Introduction

Angela was born in Foligno, Italy, twenty-four years after Francis of Assisi's death. Little is known of her early years except that she came from a prosperous family. We first encounter Angela as a thirty-seven-year-old married woman. She is described as intelligent, well-educated, a socialite who "colored and braided" her hair, wore shoes "adorned with cut leather," and "studied that she might obtain the fame of sanctity." In her writings Angela admits to performing good deeds to impress her friends and associates. Outwardly, she would appear austere, but at night Angela confessed that she "had many sheets and coverings where she lay down to sleep, causing them to be taken away in the morning that none might see them."[1]

In 1285, after reflecting on her deceitfulness and dishonesty, Angela became repentant. "As I walked by the way of penitence," Angela tells us, "I did take eighteen spiritual steps before I came to know the imperfection of my life."[2] At this time Angela experienced a sudden conversion. Then after her husband's death she joined the Franciscan Tertiaries, a lay group dedicated to living according to the spirit of St. Francis of Assisi.

Meditating on the Passion of Christ helped Angela divest herself of material possessions such as her pretty clothes, rich food and beautiful things. She felt that she must detach herself from all human attachments, even her family. So when her husband, her mother, and her sons all died within a short time of one another, Angela, though deeply grieved at their tremendous loss, was able to let go and share her experience of detachment with us:

In this beholding of the Cross I did so burn with the fire of love and remorse, that standing before it I did divest myself of everything and thus offer myself to Him....There was given to me the desire to seek out and know the way of this Cross that I might stand at its foot and find refuge there....Unto that end I was enlightened and instructed after this manner; that if I did desire to find the way and come unto the Cross, I must first pardon all those who had offended me and must then put away all earthly things, not only out of my affections but likewise in very deed, and all men and women, friends and kindred and every other thing, but more especially my possessions must I put away, even my own self. And I must give my heart to Christ, electing to walk upon the thorny path which is the path of tribulation.[3]

With her emphasis on poverty and the passionate love of the crucified Christ, Angela reflected Franciscan spirituality in her teachings.

Describing the mystical life as a sequence of seven steps culminating in her vision of herself in God, Angela heard God speak: "In you rests all the Trinity, all Truth, so that you hold Me and I hold you."[4] Her mystical visions were recorded by her Franciscan confessor and later became known as the *Book of Visions and Instructions*.

Angela became seriously ill in September 1308. She called her spiritual family around her, laid hands on each of them, and blessed them with these words: "It hath pleased the Divine Goodness," she said "to give into my care all His sons and daughters in this world, both here and beyond the seas. I have cared for them and suffered for them and my sufferings have been greater than you would believe. O my God! this day I give them back to Thee that Thou keep them and preserve them from all ill."[5]

Angela died on January 4, 1309. She was beatified in 1693, and her feast day is January 4.

Reflection

There was a time, we read, when my soul was exalted to behold God with so much clearness that never before had I beheld him so distinctly. But love did I not see here so fully; rather did I lose that which before I had and was left without love. Afterwards did I see him darkly, and this darkness was the greatest blessing that could be imagined and no thought could conceive aught that would equal this.

Then was there given unto the soul an assured faith, a firm and certain hope, wherein I felt so sure of God that all fear left me. For by that blessing which came with the darkness I did collect my thoughts and was made so sure of God that I can never again doubt but that I do of a certainty possess him.[6]

Discussion Starters

1. As you reflect on your own suffering and the suffering of others, where do you see God being revealed in it?

2. What difference does it make for you to believe that God is present during times of darkness when you feel like you are in a "spiritual desert," unable to experience the divine presence in your life?

3. How have you experienced the love of God through the caring of family, friends, faith community, and others during the "spiritual desert" times of your life?

4. In what ways has your faith grown through times of spiritual and emotional pain such as uncertainty? tribulation? stress? loneliness? boredom?

Prayer Experiences

1. Relax by taking several deep breaths. As you inhale, count slowly to three. As you exhale, count slowly to three. Become completely still.

2. Read Angela's reflection slowly and meditatively.

3. Reflect on the meaning of suffering in your life and in the lives of others. Be aware of times your faith and the faith of others has grown stronger in spite of troubles and pain. Offer thanks for these occasions of growth.

4. Reflect on times of darkness when you felt like you were in a "spiritual desert," unable to experience the divine presence in your life. Be aware of any images, feelings, thoughts, or insights that emerge. Share these responses with God in a prayerful conversation.

5. Be attentive to ways you have grown closer to God in times of emotional or spiritual struggles such as: uncertainty, tribulation, stress, loneliness, boredom, etc. Offer thanks to God for the power of divine love working in you. Offer thanks for the people who reflected God's love for you in your "spiritual desert."

6. Relax in God's extravagant love for you. Contemplate the richness and depth of this infinite love for you and for all humanity in the midst of our suffering, hurt, and pain.

7. Pray for others who suffer in "dark deserts" of the spirit. Consider ways that you can, by your loving presence, reflect God's compassionate love to those who do not experience God's presence in their lives now.

Catherine of Siena

(1347–1380)

Introduction

Catherine Benincasa was born in the Italian city of Siena, the second youngest of twenty-five children. At the age of seven she consecrated herself to Christ. She became a member of the Mantellate, a group of laywomen associated with the Dominican order, at the age of sixteen and lived in solitude in a small room in her parents' house until 1367. There she experienced a mystical marriage with Christ.

Then, in response to a divine call, Catherine began a ministry to the needy of Siena. She performed works of mercy for the poor, the sick, and prisoners. Catherine became involved in the ecclesiastical and political controversies among the Italian city-states. Catherine wrote over four hundred letters to leaders of church and state. These letters and the spiritual treatise referred to as *The Dialogue* were Catherine's gift to the Christian community.

Catherine's spirituality, as reflected in *The Dialogue*, focuses on truth, the truth about God, oneself, others, and the world: "To attain this union and purity, you must never pass judgment in human terms on anything you see or hear from anyone at all, whether it concerns you or someone else. You must consider only my will for them and for you."[1]

In *Legenda*, Raymond of Capua, Catherine's spiritual director, records the following conversation Catherine had with Christ: "Remember how you used to plan to put on man's attire and enter the Order of Preachers in foreign parts to labor for the good of souls?" Christ asks. "Why then are you surprised, why are you sad, because I am now drawing you on to the work which you have longed for from your infancy?" She protests that she is a woman, that the world has no use for women like that, that women cannot freely associate in the company of men. The Lord answers: "No thing is impossible with God.... With me there is no longer male and female ... for all stand equal in my sight, and all things are equally in my power to do."[2]

Catherine preached reform in a church filled with political and social tension. During the last five years of her life, in 1377, she persuaded Pope Gregory XI to move the papacy from Avignon to Rome. Catherine acted as an advisor to Gregory's successor, Pope Urban VI. In spite of her deliberations she was unable to prevent the Great Schism. Exhausted from her efforts to achieve reconciliation and unity, Catherine became seriously ill and died at the age of thirty-three in Rome on April 29, 1380.

In recognition of Catherine's powerful witness and leadership in the church, in 1970 Pope Paul VI gave her the title "Doctor of the Church." As a mystic activist and a peacemaker, Catherine is a mentor to women in the church today who advocate change and transformation of sexist and patriarchal structures and seek new possibilities for women in ministry.

In the following reflection, Catherine shares a vision she had of the crucified Christ.

Reflection

I saw the crucified Lord coming down to me in a great light, and for this, by the impetus of the mind that would fain go forth to meet its Creator, the body was constrained to rise. Then from the marks of his most sacred wounds, I saw five blood-red rays coming down upon me, which were directed towards the hands and feet and heart of my body. Wherefore, perceiving the mystery I straightway exclaimed: Ah, Lord my God, I beseech thee, let not the marks appear outwardly on my body! Then while I was yet speaking, before the rays reached me, they changed their blood-red colour to splendor and in the semblance of pure light they came to the five places in my body. So great is the pain that I endure sensibly in all those five places but especially within my heart, that, unless the Lord works a new miracle, it seems not possible to me that the life of my body can stay with such agony and that it will not end in a few days.[3]

Discussion Starters

1. How can you, like Catherine, be a mystic activist and a peacemaker in the church and society today?

2. Are you comfortable proclaiming a challenging message of change in church and society? Why? Why not?

3. How can groups and faith communities that advocate transformation of sexist and patriarchal structures in church and society make a difference?

4. How can reflecting on Catherine's vision of the crucified Jesus be a catalyst for change and transformation of sexist and patriarchal structures in church and society?

Prayer Experience

1. Sit in a comfortable position. Breathe slowly and consciously. For several minutes repeat the word "Jesus" as you slowly breathe in and as you breathe out as a prayerful mantra to help you become centered and peaceful.

2. Invite Catherine to preach a sermon on transforming patriarchal structures in the church and society. Listen as she reproaches the church and society for its resistance to change, for its legitimation of structures that promote the domination and subordination of women.

3. Share with Catherine any feelings of anger, frustration, or fear you have experienced in working for equality and justice in the church. You may wish to list them on paper, you may wish to shout, cry out, punch a pillow, or work with clay to express your feelings.

4. When you have finished, look at a crucifix or some other image of Jesus on the Cross. Or imagine Jesus dying on the

Cross. Contemplate the depth of Jesus' boundless, passionate love for all women in the church and society.

5. Listen as Jesus says to you: "I understand everything. I will redeem, liberate, and transform all unjust structures that oppress women in church and society." Imagine the power of Jesus' saving love transforming the church and society into the discipleship of equals where women and men live in mutuality and love and work together to promote the reign of God.

6. Ask Jesus to reveal any steps you can take to promote justice and equality in church and society. Become aware of your inner strength to work for change. Commit yourself to a specific plan of action.

7. Record any insights, feelings, thoughts, images, or sensations that emerge from your reflection in your prayer journal, in poetry, art, dance, or song, or in some other creative way.

Catherine of Genoa

(1447–1510)

Introduction

Catherine was born in 1447 into the aristocratic Fieschi family of Genoa. Little is known of her childhood except that she was devout. According to her biographers she had a remarkable spiritual experience at the age of twelve. "God in his grace bestowed on her the gift of prayer, and a wonderful communion with our Lord, which enkindled within her a new flame of deep love, together with a lively sense of the sufferings he endured in his holy passion" (*Life*, 20).[1]

After her father died, Catherine was placed in the custody of her older brother, Giacomo, who arranged a marriage for her to Giuliano Adorno, a member of another wealthy Genoese family from whom the Fieschi family was alienated. The marriage was a sign of healing for the two rival families.

The first years of marriage were indeed depressing ones for Catherine. Her husband was "entirely the opposite of herself in his mode of life" (*Life*, 22). Giuliano gambled, had a mistress, and fathered an illegitimate child. "She was a most pitiable object," comments her biographer. "She lived in a solitary house, alone, to satisfy him and never went out except to attend mass, and then as quickly as possible, for she would endure anything rather than give pain to others" (*Life*, 151).

On March 22, 1473, Catherine had a transforming spiritual experience. As she knelt before her confessor, she received a "wound to the heart" from God's infinite love and, at the same time, a deep consciousness of her own imperfections and a new awareness of the power of God's goodness. Leaving the room where her confessor was, Catherine reflected,"Oh, Love, can it be that you have called me with such love and made me to know in one instant that which tongue cannot utter?" Immediately, Catherine's depression lifted and from then on, she began a life of generous, courageous service to others. "The Spirit wanted [her] to work with human misery as if [she] were kneading bread, and even, if need be, to taste it a bit."[2]

Catherine worked with a charitable organization, the Ladies of Mercy, in the slums of Genoa, cleaning houses, and doing laundry. She served the poor wherever she found them. Catherine also worked as director of Pammetone Hospital, where she ministered to the victims of the plague that would wipe out most of Genoa's population in the late summer of 1493. Catherine organized teams of nurses, doctors, and Franciscan tertiaries throughout the summer to provide assistance to the sick and dying (*Life*, 45).

A few months after Catherine's conversion, Giuliano experienced a conversion. He joined the Third Order of St. Francis and joined Catherine in her work with the poor and needy.

During the last months of her life Catherine experienced a long, drawn-out mysterious illness. Her followers witnessed her physical agony and her exultant spirit. "They beheld heaven in her soul, and purgatory in her agonized body" (*Life*, 162).

Reflection

And the state of this soul is then a feeling of such utter peace and tranquility that it seems to her that her heart, and her bodily being, and all both within and without is immersed in an ocean of utmost peace; from which she shall never come forth for anything that can befall her in this life. And she stays immovable, imperturbable, impassible.... And she is so full of peace that though she press her flesh, her nerves, her bones, no other thing comes forth from them than peace. (Life, 18)

Discussion Starters

1. Have you ever experienced a deep awareness of God's peace? If so, what impact did this experience have on your life? If

not, what impact do you think the experience of God's peace might have on your life?

2. What people and experiences have helped you to be more at peace with God and with yourself? How is the Spirit working through you at the present time to share the gift of peace with others?

3. What can you do to open yourself more fully to God's peace?

4. How can you be an instrument of peace to the poor and needy?

Prayer Experience

1. Select some classical or instrumental music to accompany your prayer. Begin by playing the piece you selected.

2. Read Catherine's reflection aloud and slowly. Pause occasion-ally and allow images such as the soul "immersed in an ocean of utmost peace" to speak to you.

3. Look within yourself. Reflect on the people and experiences that have helped you to be more at peace with God and with yourself. Be aware of how the Spirit is working through you at the present time to share the gift of peace with others. Make a list of these or draw a symbol and fill it with words or images that describe your experience of giving and receiving peace.

4. Select one word or image that describes your experience of spiritual peace. Pray it over and over, allowing it to open you in a new way to a deeper discovery and celebration of God's peace in your life.

5. Be aware of the challenges and obstacles of daily life that may disturb your inner peace, such as the demands of spouse and children, care of elderly parents, health problems, lack of time for rest, relationships, and prayer, pressures on the job, house-hold chores, etc. Write a letter to God or Catherine of Genoa asking them how you can discover a deeper spiritual peace in the midst of the chaos (sometimes!) of your life.

6. Reflect on the values of our culture that you need to let go of in order to open yourself more fully to God's peace.

7. Think about at least one way you might be an instrument of peace to the poor, the needy, the homeless, the refugees, the imprisoned, the abused. Decide on one concrete way you will share your spiritual or material abundance with them.

Marguerite d'Oingt

(d. 1310)

—— ❧ ——

Introduction

Marguerite d'Oingt came from one of the Lyonnais's most influ-
ential families, whose history could be traced back to 1000. Yet
little biographical information is available about her except what
is contained her writings. She had two brothers and three sisters;
two of her sisters became nuns. Joining the Carthusians, a contemplative religious order, Marguerite became the fourth prioress
of the community at Poleteins in 1288. There she had profound
mystical experiences and recorded her Latin *Meditations*. In this
work, Marguerite used metaphors and visual imagery to portray a
vibrant and clear picture of her spiritual experiences. She wrote
what she felt God had written in her heart.[1]

Recalling her motives for writing, Marguerite emphasized that
she wrote because of the overwhelming power that her visionary
experiences had on her. They affected her body in such a way
that she became physically sick. She was cured only by writing
down these mystical revelations. In a letter to a friend or a spiritual director, Marguerite described the physiological effect of her
visions:

> My sweet father, I don't know if what is written in the book
> is in Holy Scripture, but I know that she who put these
> things into writing was so ravished in our Lord one night
> that it seemed to her that she saw all these things. And
> when she returned to herself, he had them all written in
> her heart in such a way that she could not think about
> anything else, but her heart was so full that she could not
> eat, nor drink, nor sleep, to the degree that she fell into
> such a great weakness that the doctors believed her close

to death.... She began to write everything that is in this
book... and as soon as she put a word in the book, it left
her heart.... And when she had written everything she was
completely cured. I firmly believe that if she had not put it in
writing she would have died or become crazy.... And this is
why I believe that this was written by the will of Our Lord.[2]

Marguerite contributed two new perspectives to visionary writing by women. She implied that the visionary herself is a text, "a
body in whom or on whom a text is inscribed." And she focused
on the act of writing: "the text written within her is physically
transferred by her to the pages of a book — 'as soon as she put
a word in that book, it left her heart.'"[3] This approach to writing considers bodily experiences as an integral part of expression
and is evident in her first work, *Pagina Meditationum*, "Page of
Meditations."

She began this book with a description of her conversion experience in 1286. While participating in the Mass, certain lines
touched her, and she began to think about them. Then she wrote
down her insights in order to contemplate them later during
prayer. While meditating on Christ's passion, she reflected on the
love of God for humanity. Near the end of this section Marguerite
described her vision of Christ as her mother: "For are you not my
mother and more than my mother?"[4] Marguerite did not desire to
have any mother or father except Christ. She asked Christ if he is
not her mother more than her mother since her mother labored
to give her birth a single day or night but Christ labored to give
her spiritual life for more than thirty years.

Reflection

*For are you not my mother and more than my mother? The mother
who bore me laboured in delivering me for one day or one night but
you, my sweet and lovely Lord, laboured for me for more than thirty
years. Ah, my sweet and lovely Lord, with what love you laboured
for me and bore me through your whole life. But when the time ap-
proached for you to be delivered, your labour pains were so great that*

your holy sweat was like great drops of blood that came out from your body and fell on the earth.... Ah! Sweet Lord Jesus Christ, who ever saw a mother suffer such a birth! For when the hour of your delivery came you were placed on the hard bed of the cross... and your nerves and all your veins were broken. And truly it is no surprise that your veins burst when in one day you gave birth to the whole world.[5]

Discussion Starters

1. How did you feel about Marguerite's image of Jesus as mother who gave birth to the whole world?

2. What new insights does Marguerite's reflection give us into the death and resurrection of Jesus Christ?

3. What experiences have you had of giving birth physically or spiritually? What images would you use to describe your experiences?

4. How has your relationship with God grown during times you have given birth (physically or spiritually) to others? to self?

Prayer Experience

(You may wish to use a crucifix or a painting of the crucifixion to draw you into this meditation. If not, use your imagination.)

1. Quiet your mind and your body. Take several deep breaths. Let go of any outside noises or distraction. Be still in the presence of Jesus.

2. Read Marguerite's reflection slowly and thoughtfully. Imagine that you are present at the Cross of Jesus. Be aware of Jesus' physical, emotional, and spiritual agony... torture... pain.... See the blood flowing from his body... the anguish of his soul... the love of his heart.... Immerse yourself totally in the depths of Jesus' sufferings. Imagine the death and resurrection of Jesus Christ giving birth to you... to others... to the whole world... in new and powerful ways.

3. Reflect on times during your life when you experienced physical illness, emotional or spiritual pain, loneliness, alienation, hurt, rejection, depression, abandonment, hostility, etc. As you remember these times, surrender each one to Jesus on the Cross. Ask Jesus to "birth" you into new life in each of these situations. As you do so, immerse yourself in the passionate, total, infinite love of Jesus for you. Observe Jesus liberating you, healing you, forgiving you, transforming you, "birthing" you ... and "birthing" others in these situations to deeper spiritual growth.

4. Be aware of any thoughts, feelings, images, or sensations that emerge during your experience of Jesus "birthing" you ... and "birthing" others to new life. Record your reflections in your prayer journal.

5. Be aware of experiences you have had of giving birth physically or spiritually to others. Offer prayers of praise and thanksgiving for these "birthing" experiences. Decide to celebrate at least one of these experiences of "new life" with others.

6. Pray for family, friends, neighbors, and the poor and suffering people of the world. Ask God to "birth" them into new life through the power of the saving death and resurrection of Jesus Christ.

7. Draw an image or symbol of one of your experiences of "birth" and "new life." Hang this in a prominent place in your home as a reminder of fresh hope and passionate love.

Julian of Norwich

(1342–1415)

Introduction

Julian of Norwich, a medieval mystic, was born in Norwich, England, in 1342. She may have attended school at the Benedictine convent at Carrow. Very little is known about her early life. She described herself as unlettered but demonstrated great literary skill in her writings. "That Julian was educated at all indicates that she was from an upper-class family, possibly from the increasingly affluent group of Norwich merchants and professionals," comments Gloria Durka in her book *Praying with Julian of Norwich.*[1]

Julian lived as an anchoress in a small room attached to the church of St. Julian in Norwich. When she was thirty, Julian suffered a serious illness. From her writings we learn that her mother was present and a parish priest administered the last rites. During her sickness, Julian had sixteen powerful revelations of God's love. She referred to these visions as "showings."

In her writings, which were rooted in the ancient contemplative tradition of the desert mothers and fathers, Julian revealed extraordinary insights into the mysteries of God's revelation to us, the power of evil, the union of humanity with Christ in the Trinity, and the final transformation of all things in God. According to Thomas Merton, Julian is a "true theologian with greater clarity, depth, and order than St. Teresa: she really elaborates, theologically, the content of her revelations."

One of her most telling and central convictions is her orientation to what one might call an eschatological secret, the hidden dynamism which is at work already and by which "all manner of things shall be well." This secret, this act which the Lord keeps hidden away, is really the full fruit of the *Parousia*. . . . Actually, her life was lived in the belief in this "secret," this "great deed" that the Lord will do on the Last Day. . . . All partial expectation will be exploded and everything will be made right.[2]

Julian, who is perhaps best-known for her development of the notion of the motherhood of God, described God's mothering activity in her *Revelations of Divine Love*. According to this mystic, divine nurturing love is expressed in a rich variety of ways: conception in the womb; the pain and trauma of labor and birth; the nurturing of the suckling child; the care and education of the older child; the bathing, healing, forgiving, guiding, and comforting of the child as she or he grows and matures; and the loving care of the child even to the point of death and return to the original womb. Julian believed that the quality of a mother is present in the Trinity, as well that of a Father, a Son, and their Spirit. "As truly as God is our Father, so truly is God our mother. To the property of motherhood belong nature, love, wisdom and knowledge, and this is God."

Reflection

As to the first, I saw and understood that the high might of the Trinity is our Father, and the deep wisdom of the Trinity is our Mother, and the great love of the Trinity is our Lord; and all these we have in nature and in our substantial creation. . . .

Thus in our Father, God almighty, we have our being, and in our Mother of mercy we have our reforming and restoring, in whom our parts are united . . . and through the rewards and the gifts of grace of the Holy Spirit we are fulfilled. . . .

The mother can give her child a suck of milk, but our precious Mother Jesus can feed us with himself and does . . . The mother can lay her child tenderly to her breast, but our tender Mother Jesus can lead us easily into his blessed breast through his sweet open side, and show us there a part of the godhead and of the joys of heaven, with inner certainty of endless bliss.[3]

Discussion Starters

1. In what ways have you been involved in creative, nurturing relationships or activities that can be described as "mothering"?

2. What does experiencing God as mother do to your own identity as mother/nurturer/creator?

3. How are you nurtured as you nurture others?

4. How can the image of Jesus as mother enrich your relationship with Jesus?

Prayer Experience

1. Relax for a few moments in silence. Breathe slowly and deeply. As you inhale, be conscious of God's infinite love surrounding you, permeating you, filling you, transforming you, empowering you. As you exhale, breathe out God's love for you. Picture this love surrounding, permeating, filling, and transforming your relatives, friends, co-workers, neighbors, all people and all creation.

2. Read the passages from Julian slowly and meditatively. Let the images "speak" to you.

3. Reflect on times either recently or in the past when you have been involved in creative, nurturing relationships or activities that can be described as "mothering." Be aware of any thoughts, images, insights, memories, or sensations that emerge. Write down a phrase, a sentence, or an image describing each experience.

4. Imagine God as Mother nurturing you ... loving you ... empowering you with courage and strength to change unjust situations and structures ... transforming you into a creative birther of new life, fresh hope, wonderful dreams.

5. Be aware of how experiencing God as mother affects your own identity as mother/nurturer/creator. Dialogue with God about ways you can be nurturing and creative in your life now. Share

with God some of the ways you have experienced nurturing from others as you nurtured them.

6. Reflect on the impact that mothering Jesus can have on you. Have a prayerful conversation with Jesus about your need of this mothering love in your life now. As you do so, imagine Jesus nurturing you with whatever you need now to live a holy life.

7. Be aware of any thoughts, feelings, insights, images, or sensations that emerge. Draw a symbol or a mandala expressing the ways you feel the image of Jesus as mother can deepen your relationship with Jesus and enrich your spiritual life.

Teresa of Avila

(1515–1582)

Introduction

Teresa of Avila was born in Spain in 1515. She grew up during
Spain's colonization of the New World to the west. In her autobiography, Teresa describes how she persuaded her brother to go
with her to the land of the Moors to be a martyr for the faith:
"...and our Lord, I believe, had given courage enough, even at so
tender an age, if we could have found the means to proceed; but
our greatest difficulty seemed to be our father and mother" (*Autobiography*, 1:4).[1] After this plan failed, she coaxed her brother to
assist her in building hermitages in the garden. "I contrived to be
alone, for the sake of saying my prayers...I used to delight...in
the building of monasteries, as if we were nuns: I gave alms as I
could" (*Autobiography*, 1:6).[2]

As a teen, Teresa experienced some of the turmoil and temptation common to adolescents of every age. Teresa enjoyed partying
and a good time. After her mother died, Teresa's stepsister,
involved in the planning of her wedding, supervised Teresa's
activities. Teresa was exposed to some negative influences and relationships during her adolescent years. She later described her
experience: "I am amazed at the evil one bad companion can
do: the conversation of this person so changed me that no trace
was left of my soul's natural disposition to virtue" (*Autobiography*,
2:5).[3]

Teresa entered the convent of the Incarnation in Avila in 1536.
There she found a worldly atmosphere that did not help her
develop a contemplative life. During this time she reflects she
"was ashamed to draw near unto God in an act of such special
friendship as prayer" (*Autobiography*, 7:1).[4]

Then one day Teresa had a powerful vision of Christ that changed her life:

> The vision of Christ left upon me an impression of His most extraordinary beauty, and the impression remains today; one time is sufficient to make this imprint.... After I beheld the extraordinary beauty of the Lord, I didn't see anyone who in comparison with Him seemed to attract me or occupy my thoughts. By turning my gaze just a little inward to behold the image I have in my soul, I obtained such freedom in this respect that... it would be impossible for me... to be so occupied with the thought of anyone that I couldn't free myself from it by only a slight effort to remember this Lord. (*Autobiography*, 37:4)[5]

After reflecting on her own manner of living the rule, Teresa realized that it was time to make a drastic change. She decided to found another Carmel, in which the Primitive Rule of the order would be observed. On August 24, 1562, the first house of the Reform, St. Joseph, was established. In the years that followed Teresa embarked on the mission of reforming the Carmel order, despite the opposition of her own community, who considered her a rebel. Teresa established fifteen houses for the Discalced Carmelite nuns and, in collaboration with John of the Cross, two houses for the friars.

Teresa died at Alba de Tormes on October 4, 1582. She was canonized by Pope Gregory XV in 1622 and declared the first woman doctor of the church on September 27, 1970.

Teresa's writings include the following: *Autobiography, The Way of Perfection, The Foundations, Meditations on the Canticle, Visitation of the Discalced Nuns,* and *The Interior Castle.*

In *The Interior Castle,* Teresa uses the image of a mansion as a symbol of the stages in spiritual growth. Each mansion has several rooms through which the soul moves to encounter the king. The first three consist of meditation, spiritual reading, and the practice of charity. The fourth focuses on the prayer of quiet. The fifth and sixth present the state of infused contemplation. In the sixth mansion the soul meditates on the humanity of Christ. The seventh stage describes the experience of mystical marriage.

Reflection

We cannot know whether or not we love God, although there are strong indications for recognizing that we do love God; but we can know whether we love our neighbor. And be certain that the more advanced you see you are in love for your neighbor the more advanced you will be in the love of God.[6]

Discussion Starters

1. How do you experience God's presence in your family? friends? co-workers? boss? strangers? neighbors?

2. Do you agree with Teresa's assertion that "the more advanced you are in love for your neighbor the more advanced you will be in love for God"? Why? Why not?

3. What obstacles, if any, keep you from loving your neighbor?

4. In what ways are you being called by God to lovingly care for your family, friends, co-workers, boss, strangers, neighbors, etc.?

Prayer Experience

1. Take a few minutes of silence to become quiet and relaxed. Imagine that you are on an elevator descending slowly from the twentieth floor. 20...19...18...15...11...7...5...3...2...1...

2. Read the passage from Teresa of Avila slowly and carefully.

3. Reflect on the ways that you experience God's presence in your family ... friends ... co-workers ... boss ... strangers ... neighbors..., etc. Offer thanks for each person who comes to mind.

4. Become aware of any obstacles or blockages that keep you from loving others. Make a list of these concerns. As you write each one, surrender it into the infinite ocean of God's mercy. See each obstacle transformed into an occasion of grace.

5. As you do this, become conscious of any feelings that emerge. You may wish to record these in your prayer journal.

6. Make a list of people you feel God is calling you to serve at the present time. Imagine yourself in the presence of each "neighbor." Ask each person how can you love him or her more deeply. Listen to each one's response.

7. Now visualize the infinite love of God flowing through you as you lovingly care for and generously serve each person's needs. Be aware of any changes that occur in your attitudes toward serving your neighbors. Decide on one act of loving service you will perform for your neighbors.

Jane Frances de Chantal

(1572–1641)

Introduction

Jeanne-Françoise Frémyot de Chantal was born into a wealthy family of Dijon, France, on January 23, 1572. Her mother died when she was a child so Jane was raised by her father, who made sure that the skills, intelligence, and abilities of his daughter were developed.

She married at twenty to a baron, Christophe de Rabutin Baron de Chantal. They enjoyed a loving and happy relationship. They had seven children, four of whom lived to adulthood. In 1600, after eight years of marriage, the baron was accidentally killed in a hunting accident. Then Jane lived with her husband's family, raised her children, and served the poor.

In 1604, after hearing a sermon of Francis de Sales, bishop of Geneva, Jane began what was to become a close spiritual friendship with the bishop. Jane reflected Francis's spirituality of gentleness in her writings. She shared the following advice with one of her sisters: "No matter what happens, be gentle with yourself."

In 1610, Jane and Francis together founded an order devoted to visiting the poor and sick, known as the Order of the Visitation of Mary. This was a new form of religious life for women, who until this time had been required to be enclosed in a cloister and whose active ministry had been limited to the education of girls. This pioneering community would be devoted to prayer and to charitable service. The Visitation was open to women who wished to live a religious life without being enclosed in a cloister. However, due to the opposition of church officials such as Cardinal de Marquermont, who demanded that the order be enclosed in order to received ecclesiastical approbation, the Visitation became an enclosed order for the education of young girls. At the time of Jane's death on December 13, 1641, there were over eighty houses of the order.[1]

Jane and a small group of women often met with Francis de Sales in the garden of Annecy to discuss the nature of the contemplative life. It was from these conversations that Francis's book on spirituality was formed — *The Treatise on the Love of God*. According to author Wendy M. Wright, this work was also Jane's book because "it was his contact with her that had first hinted to him of the rich possibilities of the life of prayer and his continuing friendship with her that confirmed those first intimations." As friends and companions Jane and Francis offered each other mutual support in their spiritual journey.[2]

Jane Frances de Chantal was canonized in 1767, and her feast is celebrated in the United States on August 18.

The following reflections are taken from conferences she gave her sisters.

Reflection

When you have committed some fault, go to God humbly, saying to him, "I have sinned, my God, and I am sorry." Then, with loving confidence, add: "Father, pour the oil of your bountiful mercy on my wounds, for you are my only hope; heal me." A little later: "By the help of your grace, I shall be more on my guard and will bless you eternally," and speak like this according to the different movements and feelings of your soul. Sometimes put yourself very simply before God, certain of his presence everywhere, and without any effort, whisper very softly to his sacred heart whatever your own heart prompts you to say.

When you are experiencing some physical pain or a sorrowful heart, try to endure it before God, recalling as much as you can that he is watching you at this time of affliction, especially in physical illness when very often the heart is weary and unable to pray. Don't force yourself to pray, for a simple adherence to God's will, expressed from time to time, is enough. Moreover, suffering borne in the will quietly and patiently is a continual, very powerful prayer before God.[3]

Discussion Starters

1. How would you describe the way you pray at this time?

2. In what ways could Jane de Chantal's reflection on prayer enrich your prayer life?

3. Do you believe that suffering "born in the will quietly and patiently" is a very powerful prayer? Why? Why not? How has your experience of suffering affected your prayer?

4. How has prayer helped you to experience God's healing of failure in your life?

Prayer Experience

1. Begin this prayer experience by inhaling God's tremendous love. Exhale any negative feelings or thoughts. Imagine God's faithful love within you and all around you.

2. Read Jane de Chantal's reflection slowly and prayerfully.

3. Have a "heart to heart" conversation with God. Share your hopes, fears, dreams, challenges, relationships, concerns, and disappointments as openly as you can. Talk to God as you would your best friend, sincerely, honestly, and lovingly.

4. Listen to what God may wish to share with you. Record key insights from this conversation in your prayer journal.

5. Reflect on your past failures. As you become aware of each sin or weakness, admit your failure, confess your sorrow, and ask God to heal you. You may wish to use Jane's words as a prayerful mantra to repeat over and over as you become conscious of your failures and sins:

> "I have sinned, my God, and I am sorry for _____ [name your failure or sin]."

> "Father, pour the oil of your bountiful mercy on my wounds, for you are my only hope, heal me. _____ [describe what needs healing]."

6. Reflect on suffering as a powerful form of prayer. Recall times of suffering in your life when you found it difficult to pray because of physical or emotional suffering. Be aware that suffering "born in the will quietly and patiently" is a very powerful prayer. Offer thanks for any growth you experienced during past times of suffering.

7. Like rays of sunshine patiently coaxing flowers to blossom, imagine the compassionate love of God helping you to grow spiritually in the midst of your failures and weaknesses. As you do so, be aware of any thoughts, feelings, or images that emerge. Design and draw a symbol of the spiritual growth that has occurred in your life because God has loved you in your failures and weaknesses.

Mary Ward
(1585–1645)

Introduction

Mary Ward was born in 1585 in York, England, during a time of dangerous persecution. Mary founded the Institute of the Blessed Virgin Mary, the first unenclosed order for active women religious in the Roman Catholic Church. This first experiment of active women religious, vowed to poverty, chastity, and obedience, modeled their rule and spirituality on those of St. Ignatius of Loyola. Mary adapted the Jesuit Formula Instituti and modeled her community after the Society of Jesus as women contemplatives in action.

Dealing with new questions and developing new roles for women in religious life, Mary Ward described the tensions that occurred with church officials:

> Diverse [women] followed with intention to be religious where I should be, living together there. Great insistence was made by diverse spiritual and learned men that we would take upon us some rule already confirmed. Several rules were procured by our friends, both from Italy and France, and we earnestly urged to make choice of some of them. They seemed not that which God would have done and the refusal of them caused much persecution, and the more, because I denied all and could not say what in particular I desired or found myself called unto.[1]

Mary Ward's prophetic vision challenged an old institution to open itself to new understandings. In an age whose only concept of religious life for women was enclosure in a monastery, church officials did not want women on the streets feeding the hungry, comforting the sick, teaching children or doing anything else outside the cloister. Undaunted by the harsh criticism of her detractors, who labelled her followers "jesuitesses," Mary walked from Brussels to Rome to meet with Pope Gregory XV in 1621. During the time she anxiously hoped for her Institute's approval, her community continued to grow.

In the following letter Mary Ward expressed her loneliness and her desire to do God's will with her Institute:

> I then offered myself to suffer with love and gladness whatsoever trouble or contrariety should happen in my doing his will, but besought him withal that none of those things might hinder what his will was to have done. Presented [with the possibility] that perchance there was some great trouble to happen about the confirmation of our course, with this I found a great and new love for this Institute and a near embracing or union of affection with it. I offered myself willingly to this difficulty and besought our Lord with tears that he would give me grace to bear it, and no contradiction might hinder his will (whatever his will, for I had then a greater love to his will in general than to any particular).[2]

However, in 1631, with three hundred sisters in the Institute, Pope Urban VII suppressed her community. Mary was condemned as a heretic and imprisoned by the Inquisition. Even though all houses were closed, a few members stayed together, professing private vows.

Mary Ward died in 1645 and was buried in a Protestant cemetery at Osbaldwick, England. Her tombstone reads: "To love the poor, persevere in the same, live, die, and rise with them was all the aim of Mary Ward who, having lived 60 years and 8 days died the 30th of Jan. 1645." In time the Institute grew and received papal approval. In 1909 the Institute and the Sisters of Loretto would at last honor Mary Ward as its founder. In 1978 the Institute was finally permitted to realize the vision of Mary Ward: taking the constitutions of the Society of Jesus as its rule of life.[3]

Reflection

But perhaps you think women are not to preach, therefore their words are not to be regarded. It is certain that the words of everyone whosoever, man or woman, that by their place are to speak, are to be regarded, and every word, though never so little esteemed, let it not pass as if spoken by chance. It is good to take every word and action that cometh from anyone soever, who hath cause to speak, as from God.

There is no such difference between men and women; yet women, may they not do great matters as we have seen by example of many saints who have done great things? And I hope in God it will be seen that women in time will do much.[4]

Discussion Starters

1. What does Mary Ward's vision for women mean today ("And I hope in God it will be seen that women in time will do much")?

2. What is the relation of religious life to contemporary society? to the women's movement? to ministry?

3. What is your vision for women in ministry in the contemporary church?

4. For women: In what ways do you minister in the church? community? workplace? family? neighborhood? world? What difference does your ministry make? What are your hopes and dreams for your ministry in the future? For men: In what ways do you see your ministry as the same as or different from women in the church? in the community? workplace? family? neighborhood? world? What are your hopes and dreams for your ministry in the future?

Prayer Experience

1. Spend a little time in stillness. Be aware that God dwells in the still point of your being, lavishing you with overflowing love.

2. Read Mary Ward's words several times. Select a line that touches you. Repeat the line several times to reflect more deeply on its meaning.

3. Recall how you have experienced God's gracious love through women who have ministered to you. List the names of these women, beginning with those closest to you. Offer thanks for each woman that comes to mind. Choose one to whom you will write a letter of appreciation.

4. Compose a litany of praise for great women in the Scriptures and Christian tradition who have revealed God's prophetic presence in our midst, for example:

> We praise you for Sarah, mother of the chosen people.
>
> We praise you for Miriam, a leader of God's people, and partner in ministry with her brother Moses.
>
> We praise you for Ruth and Naomi, witnesses to loving friendship between women.
>
> We praise you for Deborah, judge and prophet.
>
> We praise you for Esther, courageous queen and risk-taker.
>
> We praise you for Mary, mother of Jesus, disciple and mother for all Christians.
>
> We praise you for Mary Magdalene, apostle to the apostles and first witness to the resurrection.
>
> We praise you for Phoebe, Priscilla, Lydia, Damaris, Junia, Julia, Mary, Persis, Tryphena, Tryphosa, and all of the women who were church leaders, official teachers, missionaries, and ministers of the gospel in the Christian community.
>
> We praise you for Hildegard of Bingen, German mystic, writer, abbess, scientist, and poet.

> We praise you for Julian of Norwich, English anchoress and mystic, who proclaimed God's motherly love for us and assured us "all shall be well."
>
> We praise you for St. Elizabeth Seton, wife, widow, mother, foundress of the Sisters of Charity and first American saint.
>
> We praise you for Mary Ward, woman of courage, who in spite of persecution and opposition lived her vision for women in the church.
>
> We praise you for _____ , etc.

5. Draw a mandala of your vision of women in ministry in the contemporary church. Open yourself to God's Spirit dwelling in the depths of your being. When you are ready, fill your circle with the vision that emerges from the center of your being. You may want to draw a symbol instead of a mandala.

6. If you are a woman, list the ways you minister in the church, community, workplace, family, neighborhood, world. Be aware of your ideas, insights, hopes, dreams, and new possibilities for ministry that may be available now and in the future. Ask Holy Wisdom to help you make wise choices in your present and future ministry. If you are a man, ask women whom you know to share with you their vision of ministry in the church, community, workplace, family, neighborhood, and world. Dialogue with them about your ideas, insights, hopes, dreams, and new possibilities for ministry that may be available now and in the future.

7. Write a prayer of commitment to your ministry. Place it where you will remember to pray it often. Share it with others.

Elizabeth Bayley Seton

(1774–1821)

Introduction

Elizabeth Bayley Seton was born in New York on August 28, 1774. She was raised in a wealthy Episcopalian family. Her parents had three children. Elizabeth's mother, Catherine Charlton, died when Elizabeth was three. When her father, Dr. Richard Bayley, remarried, Elizabeth inherited six new siblings. In 1794, Elizabeth married a prominent shipping merchant, William McGee Seton. Together they had five children: Anna Maria, William, Richard, Catherine, and Rebecca. While on a business trip in Italy, William Seton became ill with tuberculosis. Elizabeth and daughter Anna Maria journeyed to Pisa to be with their "beloved Will" in his illness. However, William's condition deteriorated, and he died in 1803. After her husband's death, Elizabeth stayed with the Filicci family for several months. There she developed a desire for the Eucharist and an interest in Catholicism. She returned to New York in June 1804 and became a Roman Catholic in March 1805. Coping with the death of her young husband and later of two of her children, along with misunderstanding and loss of her family fortune because of her Catholic conversion, were painful yet growthful events in Elizabeth's life-occasions of grace.

Elizabeth's letters and journals reveal a strong devotion to the Eucharist. In her journal she writes: "With what grateful and unspeakable joy and reverence I adore the daily renewed virtue of that Word by which we possess him in our blessed Mass and Communion."[1] Elizabeth's correspondence also reflects her love and concern for her own children and for all the children entrusted to her care.

In 1808 Elizabeth moved to Baltimore, and in 1809, with the

strong support of Bishop Carroll of Maryland, she founded the American Sisters of Charity and the first American Catholic schools. Her sisters founded orphanages, hospitals, and schools. At the time of her death at forty-six, her new congregation numbered twenty communities in the United States. Her letter to Rose Stubbs states clearly her vision and charism: "a religious life devoted to the education of poor children in the Catholic faith."

Elizabeth died in 1821 at Emmitsburg, Maryland. In 1903 James Cardinal Gibbons initiated proceedings for the cause of her canonization. On a beautiful sunny day in Rome, September 14, 1975, Pope Paul VI declared Elizabeth Bayley Seton the first native-born American Roman Catholic saint.[2]

Reflection

This is a Mystery, the greatest of all my stories. Not that my adored Lord is in the Blessed Sacrament of the Altar. His word has said it, and what is so simple as to take that word, which is the Truth itself? . . . Jesus then is there. We can go, receive him, he is our own. Were we to pause and think of this thro' Eternity, yet we can only realize it by his conviction: that he is there (O heavenly theme!) is as certainly true as that Bread naturally taken removes my hunger. So this Bread of Angels removes my pain, my cares, warms, cheers, soothes, contents and renews my whole being. Merciful God, and I do possess you, kindest, dearest Friend, every affection of my Nature absorbed in you still is Active, nay perfected in their operations thro' your refining love.[3]

Discussion Starters

1. Describe your experience of Christ's presence in the Eucharist.

2. What relationship do you see between the Eucharist and the Christian community? What relationship do you see between the Eucharist and your everyday life?

3. How can Elizabeth Seton's reflection help you contemplate the Eucharist?

4. In what ways does the Eucharist call you to work for justice locally and globally?

Prayer Experience

1. Close your eyes. Become aware of your breathing. As you breathe in become aware of the air flowing through your nostrils and filling your lungs. As you breathe out, release any tension or stress that you may be feeling.

2. Read Elizabeth Seton's reflection in a quiet and leisurely manner. Spend some time contemplating the mystery of Christ's presence in the Eucharist.

3. Be aware of the ways you have experienced the power of Christ's death and resurrection in the Eucharist saving, healing, and transforming you as you worshiped in the Christian community. As you do so, be conscious of any images, thoughts, feelings, or insights that emerge. You may wish to record these in your prayer journal or in poetry, song, dance, or art.

4. Reflect on the Eucharist as a meal of unity that brings together people of different races, nations, and ethnic backgrounds to celebrate their oneness with one another in Christ. Decide on one way you will foster unity and community in your family, neighborhood, city, church, country or world.

5. Celebrate the Eucharist in your local community with a deeper openness to Christ's presence in the assembly, the Word of God, the eucharistic species, and the presider. Be conscious that when the community celebrates Eucharist, the Body of Christ (the People of God) receive and become more who they already are: the Body of Christ.

6. The banquet of the Eucharist leads us to compassionate, loving service of others: including our family, friends, neighbors, co-workers, the poor, the needy, the homeless, and the refugees. Ask God to reveal ways you can serve others and work for justice locally and globally.

7. Offer thanks for the wondrous gift of the Eucharist in your life, church, and world. The next time you attend Eucharist, offer all people, your family, friends, neighbors, the poor, the needy, the homeless, the refugees, and the whole world to be transformed by the power of Christ's death and resurrection. As you do so, imagine all people being changed into the Body of Christ, radiant images of God's presence in the world.

Thérèse of Lisieux

(1873–1897)

—— ✝ ——

Introduction

Thérèse Martin, the ninth child of Louis Martin and Zelie Guerin, was born in the Normandy town of Alençon on January 2, 1873. Thérèse was the fifth daughter and last child of Louis and Zelie Martin. She was brought up in a loving, pious, middle-class family. "My earliest recollections are of tender caresses and smiles," Thérèse described her close-knit family life later. "I was always cherished with the most loving care."[1]

Thérèse expressed an interest in spiritual mysteries at a young age. Her mother's letters to Pauline, Thérèse's sister, describe Thérèse asking questions about heaven before she was three years old.

When her mother died, Thérèse was only four years old. At this time her personality changed from being vivacious, lively, and inquisitive to being shy, withdrawn, sensitive, and fearful.

Until about thirteen, Thérèse tended to be scrupulous:

All my most simple thoughts and actions became the cause of trouble for me and I had relief only when I told them to Marie. This cost me dearly, for I believed I was obliged to tell her the absurd thoughts I had even about her. As soon as I laid down my burden, I experienced peace for an instant; but this peace passed away like a lightning-flash, and soon my martyrdom began over again. (*Story*, 84–85)[2]

One Christmas thirteen-year-old Thérèse overheard her father tell Celine, her older sister, that he hoped this would be the last Christmas he would have to fill the younger children's shoes with small gifts and candy. Celine knew Thérèse would cry if she went downstairs to open the gifts after hearing this, so she advised Thérèse not to open the gifts until she had calmed down. However something special happened to Thérèse. Later she would describe this important turning point in her life in her autobiography. "I felt charity slip into my soul, and the need to forget myself and to please others. I descended the stairs rapidly; controlling the poundings of my heart, I took my slippers and placed them in front of Papa, and withdrew the objects joyfully." That night, she reflected, "began the third period of my life, the most beautiful and the most filled with graces from heaven" (Story, 98).

At fourteen Thérèse described her consciousness of her vocation to the Carmelite order, "the divine call was becoming so insistent that had it been necessary for me to go through flames to follow Our Lord, I would have cast myself into the flames" (Story, 106).

All Thérèse dreamed about was entering Carmel. Her sisters Pauline and Celine supported Thérèse's decision, but Marie thought she was too young. When Thérèse asked her father, both of them wept as they walked in the garden. Her father "cried out that God was giving him a great honor in asking his children from him." Then picking a white flower gently from a moss, "He gave it to me explaining the care with which God brought it into being and preserved it to that very day." As Thérèse took the lovely flower in her hand, she noticed that the roots were still present. This was to show that it was "destined to live on in another soil more fertile than the tender moss where it had spent its first days" (Story, 108).

Even though she encountered opposition from the bishop and the father superior of the Carmelite order, Thérèse persisted. She journeyed to Rome and asked Pope Leo XIII, who told her she would enter "if it was God's will." On New Year's day, Thérèse received a letter of acceptance from the mother superior. On March 9, 1888, at fifteen, Thérèse's dream became a reality. She entered the Carmelite convent at Lisieux:

> My soul experienced a peace so sweet, so deep, it would be impossible to express it. For seven years and a half that inner

peace has remained my lot, and has not abandoned me in
the midst of the greatest of trials.... Everything thrilled me;
I felt as though I was transported into a desert; our little
cell, above all, filled me with joy.... With what deep joy I
repeated those words: "I am here forever." (*Story*, 148)

Thérèse devoted her life in Carmel to living her "little way" of
spiritual perfection. At the request of her prioress, Thérèse began
writing her autobiography, *The Story of a Soul*, in 1894. This book
focused on paying attention to the small, ordinary things in life.
In it she wrote:

Instead of becoming discouraged, I said to myself: God cannot inspire unrealizable desires. I can, then, in spite of my
littleness, aspire to holiness. It is impossible for me to grow
up, and so I must bear with myself such as I am with all my
imperfections. But I want to seek out a means of going to
heaven by a little way, a way that is very straight, very short,
and totally new. (*Story*, 297)

Thérèse suffered great pain from tuberculosis and died in 1897
when she was twenty-four years old. Pope Pius XI canonized her
on May 17, 1925.

Reflection

*Just as a torrent, throwing itself with impetuosity into the ocean,
drags after it everything it encounters in its passage, in the same way,
O Jesus, the soul who plunges into the shoreless ocean of your love,
draws with her all the treasures she possesses. Lord, you know it, I
have no other treasures than the souls it has pleased You to unite to
mine* (Story, 254).

*My way is all of trust and love, I don't understand souls who are
afraid of so loving a Friend. Sometimes, when I read spiritual treatises,
in which perfection is shown with a thousand obstacles in the way and
a host of illusions round about it, my poor little mind grows very soon
weary, I close the learned book, which leaves my head muddled and my
heart parched, and I take the holy scripture. Then all seems luminous,*

a single word opens up infinite horizons to my soul, perfection seems easy; I see that it is enough to realize one's nothingness, and give ourself wholly, like a child, into the arms of the good God.[3]

Discussion Starters

1. From Thérèse's passage and your reflections upon it, what did you learn that can enrich your spiritual journey?

2. How can relating to God as a Friend and Lover draw you into a deeper intimacy with God?

3. How can an awareness of God's loving presence help you to give yourself "wholly, like a child, into the arms of the good God"?

4. In what ways are our world and church being challenged to grow in a deeper trust in God? In what ways are you being challenged to grow in a deeper trust in God now?

Prayer Experience

1. Breathe deeply, rhythmically, and slowly through your nose so that the abdomen rises as you inhale and lowers as you exhale through your mouth. Become aware of God's loving presence in the depths of your being.

2. Read Thérèse's reflection slowly and prayerfully.

3. Reflect on the meaning of this passage for your life now. Be aware of any thoughts, feelings, images or insights that emerge. Record these in your prayer journal.

4. Let go and let God love you completely and totally as you are at this moment in your life. Spend time in the presence of God, your Lover and Friend. Share your feelings with God. Listen as God describes how deeply you are loved.

5. Compose a poem or prayer, draw or create a piece of art, sing or dance with delight. Express in whatever way feels most appropriate God's love for you and your love for God.

6. Select one phrase from the Bible that reminds you of God's loving presence and provident care — e.g., "Arise my love, my fair one, and come away" (Song of Songs 2:10); "the Mighty one has done great things for me" (Luke 1:49); "do not fear, only believe" (Luke 8:50); "if in my name you ask me for anything I will do it" (John 14:14); "but you will receive power when the Holy Spirit has come upon you" (Acts 1:8, NRSV) — and repeat it over and over as a mantra.

7. Surrender all your cares, concerns, worries, anxieties, failures, successes, and relationships "into the arms of the good God." As you do so, pray for a deeper trust in God for yourself, the church, and the world.

Evelyn Underhill

(1875–1941)

Introduction

Evelyn Underhill was born into an upper-class family in Wolverhampton, England, on December 6, 1875. Her father and mother were agnostics who did not attend church. At sixteen Evelyn described her mother as the ideal of what a woman should be: "My ideal of a woman is that she should be clever, vivacious, accurately but not priggishly informed, gentle, truthful, tactful and tolerant, and should have a due sense of proportion. I have never met or read of anyone exactly like this, but in real life my own mother comes nearest to it."[1] She shared her father's interest in the legal profession. One of the earliest photographs of the family shows Evelyn at twelve on board the family yacht, *Amoretta*. Her father, Sir Arthur, and her mother, Lucy, are wearing yachting caps; Sir Arthur's hand is on the tiller, Mrs. Underhill holds the boat's mascot, and little Evelyn sits with a book in her hand.[2]

Educated at King's College, Evelyn displayed a keen intellect and interest in great writers such as Shakespeare, Milton, Tennyson, and Keats. In addition, she studied languages, botany, philosophy, and social science. She loved books and poetry. Her first book, *The Bar-Lamb's Ballad Book*, was published in 1902, and her first novel, *The Grey World*, was published in 1904.

While on retreat in a Catholic convent in 1907, Evelyn experienced a sudden religious conversion that convinced her of the truth of the Catholic faith. In a letter to Father Robert Hugh Benson, Evelyn wrote: "After Holy Week, and much time given to considering the question, I felt practically certain that I must eventually become a Catholic if I was to be true to my convictions."[3] But when the papal encyclical *Pascendi* condemned

Modernism, which she favored, she decided to accept spiritual homelessness rather than choose any other home than Rome.

Her spiritual struggles resulted in the publication in 1911 of *Mysticism*, which reflected a comprehensive approach to religious experience. For Evelyn Underhill the mystics are our wonderful forerunners on the journey to the Real:

> The mystics are the pioneers of the spiritual world, and we have no right to deny validity to their claims merely because we lack the courage necessary to those who would prosecute such explorations of themselves. A certain type of mind has always discerned three straight and narrow ways going out towards the Absolute: in religion, in pain, in beauty with the ecstasy of artistic satisfaction. Down these three paths as well as by many another secret way, they claim that news comes to the self-concerning levels of reality, which in their wholeness are inaccessible to the senses: worlds wondrous and immortal whose existence is not conditioned by the "given" world which those senses report.[4]

Evelyn married Hubert Moore, whom she had met as a teen and with whom she shared a love of nature, an interest in exploring old castles and churches, and the fun of making things together. Margaret Cropper, Evelyn's biographer, provides a penetrating analysis of the young couple's relationship:

> She wants his company, that is clear enough and depends on his sympathy with her over the things that she is seeing and doing. Her letters to Hubert are rather puzzling... but Evelyn was perhaps already aware of the Mystic's device, "my secret to myself." Did she perhaps cling all the closer to the staunch affection which claimed no entry into her inner life because that life was to be so cloudy and tempested, so dizzying in its snow-bound heights, so sudden in its ascents and descents that even from the first she felt the need of a plain domestic path to counterbalance the other?[5]

Under the direction of Baron Friedrich von Hügel, who became her spiritual director in 1921, Evelyn began participating fully in the sacramental life of the Church of England. At that time also she became a popular spiritual director and lecturer. She was the first woman to present theological lectures at Oxford University (1921), and she was honored as a fellow at Kings College, Cambridge in 1928. In 1938 Evelyn received the degree of doctor of divinity from Aberdeen University. In her later years, she wrote and conducted retreats; before World War II she became a pacifist. She died on June 15, 1941, in Hampstead, England. On the liturgical calendar of the Episcopal Church Evelyn is described as a "mystic and theologian."

Reflection

Not when you stand by us as an explanation of life, but when you enter our life with all its homely limitations, as friend and guest. Come in to abide with us, accepting what we have to offer; when the mysterious pilgrim passing through the world who always seems to be going further than we are, towards a strange, unknown destination — turns a chance meeting into something far deeper and closer, something we can never describe and never forget.

Lord! Give me courage and love to open the door and constrain you to enter, offer all my resources, whatever the disguise you come in, even before I fully recognize my guest.

Come in! Enter my small life!

Lay your sacred hands on all the common things and small interests of that life and bless and change them. Transfigure my small resources, make them sacred. And in them give me your very self.

When out of the heart of my own homely circumstances, you feed me — then my eyes are open to the presence I long for and can never understand.[6]

Discussion Starters

1. Have you ever experienced a deep longing for God?

2. How have you experienced God as friend in your life?

3. What obstacles prevent you from recognizing God's presence in the ordinary events of your life?

4. How would your life be different now if you were to "act as if" God is your best friend?

Prayer Experience

1. Select some classical or instrumental music to accompany your reflection. Begin by playing the piece you selected. Surround yourself with quiet and peace.

2. Read the reflection slowly and thoughtfully.

3. Consider the ways that Evelyn Underhill's experience of intimate friendship with God relates to your experience of God's friendship in your life. Reflect on a time when you experienced a longing for God's presence in your life. Share your thoughts and feelings with God about this experience. Listen to God's response. Record in your prayer journal any insights, feelings, or images that emerge from this dialogue.

4. Be conscious of your longing for friendship with God now. Allow your desire for God to pray deeply within you. As you do so, feel yourself relax in God's loving presence as you would before a close friend.

5. Now open yourself as fully as possible to God's longing for friendship with you. Be aware of any new ways God shows love, tenderness, healing, or compassion for you.

6. Be aware of any obstacles that prevent you from recognizing God as friend in the ordinary, mundane events of your life, such as stress, fatigue, difficult relationships, illness, grief, success, failure, birth or death of family members. Let go of these obstacles as you become aware of them.

7. Have a heart-to-heart conversation with God. Image God as your best friend blessing, changing, transforming the "common things and small interests" of your daily life and carrying you during the difficult, painful times. Choose to live "as if" God is your best friend now. Reflect on what a difference this would make in your relationship with God, yourself, others, the earth, all creation.

Edith Stein

(1891–1942)

Introduction

Edith Stein was born into a devout Jewish family on October 12, 1891. She was the youngest of eleven children. At the age of fifteen, according to her own recollection, Edith was not interested in God. Like many adolescents she simply forgot about God. This lack of interest lasted until she was twenty-four. Then after finishing her doctoral studies under the direction of Edmund Husserl, Edith became aware of an inner longing for God. In 1917, she earned a doctorate with her dissertation "On the Problem of Empathy." Since she was unsuccessful in securing a teaching position, Edith worked for Husserl as a research assistant for awhile but quit in frustration when this did not work out as she planned. Edith then decided to give lectures, becoming a well-known and popular speaker in Germany, Switzerland, and Austria.

In 1921, Edith came across a copy of Teresa of Avila's *The Book of Her Life* while visiting friends. Immediately, everything that she thought and believed seemed to come together and lead her to become Catholic. Edith was baptized on January 1, 1922. Edith hoped to enter Carmel right away but postponed this step because of her mother's discomfort with her conversion to Catholicism. So she lived and taught at Speyer with the Dominican sisters for eight years. After this Edith continued giving lectures in Germany and in 1933, obtained a position at the Catholic Institute for Pedagogy of Münster. However, this job did not last because of the rise of Nazism. At this time, since her only choices seemed to be either a teaching position in South America or entry into Carmel, Edith hoped that her mother would approve her choice of Carmel. So finally, on October 14, 1933 Edith entered the Carmel at Cologne. Six months later, Edith was received into religious life as a novice, becoming Sister Teresa Benedicta of the Cross.

At Cologne Edith pursued her scholarship and completed *Finite and Eternal Being*, one of her greatest philosophical writings. In 1938 she made her final profession, but within several months had to seek refuge in the Carmel at Echt in Holland. In 1942 she attempted to obtain permission to move to the Carmel at Le Paquier, Switzerland. But delays in her paperwork prevented her from escaping Nazi capture in August 1942.

Edith Stein was put to death, according to a Netherlands Red Cross report, "for reasons of race and specifically because of Jewish descent," in the gas chamber at Auschwitz on August 9, 1942.[1]

Edith's understanding of the role of woman as healer, comments Phyllis Zagano, "need not be restrained by the ordinary roles of men and women, for women may equally be united to the humanity of Christ through the mystery of the Cross. Such union can only come about if the individual is 'present, by the power of His Cross, at every front, every place of sorrow, bringing to those who suffer comfort, healing, and salvation.'"[2] As an intellectual and visionary, Edith Stein left behind a rich legacy of philosophical work and an understanding of woman that surpassed role stereotypes.

Reflection

A discerning young girl recently asked me, "Why is it that at this time so much is being said, even by men, about the nature and vocation of women?" It is astonishing how this topic is constantly being taken up by various parties, and how differently it is being treated. Leading intellectuals are painting a shining ideal of feminine nature, and they are hoping that realization of this ideal will be the cure for all contemporary ailments and needs. At the same time, in the literature of the present and of the last decades, we see woman presented again and again as the demon of the abyss. A great responsibility is being laid upon us by both sides. We are being obliged to consider the significance of woman and her existence as a problem. We cannot evade the question as to what we are and what we should be. And it is not only the reflective intellect which faces us with this question; life itself has made our existence problematic.... We have been thrown into the river, and we must swim.[3]

Discussion Starters

1. What meaning do Edith Stein's words have for women today?

2. How would you define the role of contemporary women in the family? in society? in the church?

3. How have women in the Judeo-Christian tradition enriched society and the church?

4. Name the gifts and blessings you have received from significant women in your life, such as your mother, sister, aunt, grandmother, wife, or friend.

Prayer Experience

1. Take several slow deep breaths. Be aware of places in your body where you feel stress or tension.... Take several deep breaths and breathe relaxation into each of these areas ... head ... face ... neck ... shoulders ... arms ... hands ... fingers ... back ... chest ... stomach ... pelvis ... hips ... thighs ... knees ... legs ... ankles ... feet ... toes. As you breathe in, imagine your whole body becoming radiant and energized by God's powerful Spirit. As you breathe out, imagine divine love ... forgiveness ... peace ... wisdom ... strength flowing from you to your family ... friends ... neighbors ... all people ... the earth ... the cosmos.

2. Read Edith Stein's reflection slowly and meditatively.

3. Recall the gifts and blessings you have received from significant women in your life, such as your mother, sister, aunt,

grandmother, wife, friend. List these gifts in your prayer journal and offer thanks for them. Plan a special celebration for one of these women. Send letters or gifts of appreciation to several of these women.

4. If you are a woman, write as many statements as you can beginning with "I am ...," affirming your gifts and specialness. (For example, "I am a compassionate woman." "I am a strong woman." "I am a radiant image of God's love.") If you are a man write as many statements as you can about women you know who reflect God's image to others.

5. Recall the women in the Judeo-Christian tradition who have enriched society and the church. Complete the litany below by naming the great women of the tradition for whom you want to offer thanks, or compose your own litany of thanksgiving.

> Miriam, sister of Moses and Aaron,
> > we offer thanks that with your brothers
> > you led the chosen people to freedom.
>
> Deborah, judge of Israel,
> > we offer thanks for your wisdom and justice.
>
> Mary, mother of Jesus and our mother,
> > we offer thanks for your God-bearing
> > and nurturing spirit.
>
> Talitha, daughter of Jairus,
> > we offer thanks for reminding us of Jesus' words:
> > "Fear is useless, what is needed is trust."
>
> Mary of Magdala, apostle to the apostles,
> > we offer thanks for your Easter proclamation:
> > "I have seen the Lord."
>
> Phoebe, minister to the church at Cenchreae,
> > we offer thanks for your leadership
> > in building up the Christian community.
>
> Women martyrs and mystics,
> > we offer thanks for your courage and vision.
>
> Edith Stein,
> > we offer thanks for your strength and wisdom.

6. Draw a symbol or image of your role or vocation as woman in the contemporary family, church, and society. Display it in a prominent place in your home or work site. If you are a man, ask women to share with you their feelings and insights about their role or vocation in the family, church, and society.

7. Be aware of any thoughts, feelings, insights, or images that emerge during your prayerful reflection on the role of your vocation or role as woman in family, church, or society, and on the vocation of women in contemporary life. Record these in your prayer journal.

Dorothy Day

(1897–1980)

Introduction

Dorothy Day was born in 1897 and lived in New York City, California, and Chicago. Her mother's family, who came from the Hudson Valley and Massachusetts, were boat captains, whalers, and chairmakers. Her father was a journalist, and from him Dorothy learned of the impact the written word can have on people's lives. After college, Dorothy worked as a writer for the *Liberator*, entered into a common-law marriage with Forster Batterham, had one daughter, participated in anti-war demonstrations, and was imprisoned in Washington, D.C., for her involvement in this movement. She left Forster and baptized her baby after she became a Catholic.

With Peter Maurin, Dorothy founded the Catholic Worker Movement, a ministry dedicated to a process of collaborative decision-making and to personal activism on behalf of workers. The Movement operates Houses of Hospitality in more than sixty cities in the United States as well as several farms in different areas across the country. Advocating voluntary poverty and pacifism, the spirituality of this movement is rooted in an appreciation of our dependence on God and respect for the human person. "The hallmark of both the Movement and the Houses of Hospitality is inclusiveness and respect: no one is to be made to feel like an outsider....Charity is much more than running a shelter or writing a check — and those you serve are 'ambassadors of God' who give you an opportunity to serve."[1] In 1933, the *Catholic Worker*, a newspaper to foster the vision and news of the Catholic Worker Movement, was first published.[2]

Dorothy was a realist who understood the suffering and devastation that poverty has on its victims. She realized the difficulty of preaching poverty to people living in squalor and working two jobs to make ends meet. She walked streets every day where families were evicted and furniture was piled high on the street. Dorothy recalled her experience at a city shelter: "I sat there for a couple of hours contemplating poverty and destitution in a family. Two of the children were asleep in the parents' arms and four others were sprawling against them. Another young couple were also waiting, the mother pregnant."[3]

Letting go of our attachments to material things is a painful process, Dorothy warned us. "You can strip yourself, you can be stripped but still you will reach out like an octopus to seek your own comfort, your untroubled time, your ease, your refreshment. It may mean books or music — gratification of the inner senses — or it may mean food and drink, coffee and cigarettes. The one kind of giving up is no easier than the other."[4]

For Dorothy and the Catholic Worker Movement, living the gospel meant moving away from power-grabbing, people-using, and money-chasing to serving the poor and displaced people of contemporary society. Dorothy was vividly conscious of the relationship between poverty and social justice: "One way to keep poor is not to accept money which comes from defrauding the poor."[5]

Dorothy Day died in 1980, but her legacy lives on in the people who dedicate themselves to serving the poor and destitute in soup kitchens, peace and justice centers, hospitality houses, battered women's centers, AIDS hospices, and prisons throughout the world.

Reflection

The act and spirit of giving are the best counter to the evil forces in the world today, and giving liberates the individual not only spiritually but materially. For, in a world of enslavement through installment buying and mortgages, the only way to live in any true security is to live so close to the bottom that when you fall you do not have far to drop, you do not have much to lose.

And in a world of hates and fears, we can look to Peter Maurin's words for the liberation that love brings: "Voluntary poverty is the answer. We cannot see our brother or sister in need without stripping ourselves. It is the only way we have of showing our love."[6]

Discussion Starters

1. What impact do you think Dorothy Day and the Catholic Worker Movement have had on the church and on society?

2. How can voluntary poverty liberate us from our addictions to food, alcohol, drugs, consumerism, materialism, work?

3. In your present situation how can you simplify your lifestyle, promote a deeper solidarity with the poor, and work for justice by sharing your resources with the poor?

4. In what ways can you join with others to work on solutions to structural injustices in our society such as poverty, racism, classism, sexism, ageism, and consumerism?

Prayer Experience

1. Breathe slowly and deeply several times. Become aware of each breath as you inhale and exhale. Imagine each breath you take as filled with the bountiful love of God for you and for the poor, needy, and oppressed peoples of the world.

2. Read the reflection from Dorothy Day slowly and thoughtfully.

3. Reflect on the ways you are presently involved in serving the poor, feeding the hungry, clothing the naked, sheltering the homeless, giving of yourself to others spiritually and materially. Give thanks for these opportunities to be an "ambassador of God." If there is a Catholic Worker House of Hospitality in your area, visit and talk with the residents and staff.

4. Examine your lifestyle. Review you daily relationships, activities, and habits of consumption. Consider changes you can make to simplify your lifestyle and to free yourself from

unhealthy relationships, thing-addiction, overconsumption, workaholism, materialism, consumerism.

5. Offer thanks to God for the gift of life, your body, mind, energy, time, talent, money, and all the spiritual and material resources you possess. Consider how you can be a good steward of these gifts. Make a list of some of these ways.

6. Ask God for the strength you need to be more responsive to the needs of the poor. Reflect on how you can alleviate their suffering in some way by using your personal, material, and spiritual resources.

7. Invite family, friends, neighbors, colleagues, or members of your church to join you in a justice-oriented activity. Commit yourself in solidarity with others to work for the elimination of structural injustices that keep people oppressed. As you "do justice" be aware of any thoughts, feelings, images, or insights that occur. Record these in your prayer journal.

Caryll Houselander

(1901–1954)

Introduction

Caryll Houselander was born in Bath, England, in 1901, the daughter of Willmott and Gertrude Houselander. She was baptized in the Church of England but became a Roman Catholic at the age of six. In her autobiography Caryll humorously noted that she was not a "cradle Catholic" but a "rocking horse" Catholic. Before being accepted in the church she had no instruction other than memorizing the Apostles' Creed and the Articles of Faith. However, Caryll possessed an intuitive awareness of God and was willing to believe anything she was told whether she could comprehend it or not.[1]

A year after Caryll was received into the Catholic Church, her mother became Catholic also. Then what Caryll refers to as the "persecution of piety" began. Her mother sent her to religious instructions several times a week, insisted that she recite forced prayers for priest visitors at their home, and made her attend two Masses on Sunday as well as evening benediction. Admitting this could have turned her away from orthodox religion for the rest of her life, Caryll recalled that she remained guided by an inner sense of the beauty and goodness of God. She loved to visit churches in Bristol, the city where her family had moved when she was a child. "In the presence of the Blessed Sacrament I was no longer alone, and I knew it now with the absolute certainty of a conviction that comes not from outside, but from the depths of one's own soul. I was possessed now by a longing to make my first Communion."[2]

After a long illness and bout with scrupulosity, Caryll shared a powerful experience of God's presence that removed her obsessive fears and gave her profound peace:

> It was in the evening, I think. The room was dark, and the flames of firelight dancing on the wall seemed almost to cause me pain when I opened my eyes...I no longer attempted to translate my torment as particular sins; I had realized in a dim, intuitive way that it was not something I had done that required forgiveness, but everything that I was that required to be miraculously transformed.[3]

Schooled in a Jewish kindergarten, French and English convents, a state school, a Protestant private school, St. John's Wood Art School, and St. Martin's Art School, Caryll received a comprehensive and well-rounded education. Some of her most cherished memories were spent in a French convent school in a suburb of Birmingham. Of Soeur Marie Emilie, a beloved nun, she wrote in *The Flowering Tree*:

> She has affinity with the hens.
> When a hen dies,
> she sits down on a bench and cries;
> she is the only grown-up whose tears
> are not frightening tears.
> Children can weep without shame
> at her side.[4]

As a young adult, Caryll worked in a variety of occupations: commercial artist, child-care employee, actress, letter-writer, interior decorator, and charwoman. Although finances were tight and even though she could turn to home for financial assistance, Caryll chose to live on her own and trust God: "I was confident that God whom I was forsaking, would not forsake me...and in this I was right—there was always just enough, and it was always just in time."[5]

In the years that followed Caryll became a popular author and prolific writer. She illustrated and wrote articles, verses, and stories for the *Messenger of the Sacred Heart*, the *Children's Messenger*, and the *Grail Magazine*. She had a profound awareness of Christ's presence in others and was a caring friend to people in trouble or crisis. Doctors sent their patients, both adults and children, to her for therapy and spiritual healing. Her best-sellers include these unforgettable masterpieces: *This War Is the Passion* (1941), revised as *The Comforting of Christ* (1946); *The Reed of God* (1944); *The Flowering Tree* (1945); *The Dry Wood* (1947); *The Passion of the Infant Christ* (1949); *Guilt* (1951); *The Stations of the Cross* (1955); and *The Risen Christ* (1958). Books of children's stories collected and published posthumously are *Inside the Ark* (1956), *Terrible Farmer Timson* (1957), and *Bird on the Wing* (1958).

Reflection

My cat (he is my spiritual director!) is a tabby. Just now he was in the garden when a black cat came loping along the garden wall, a very unpleasant fellow, I must admit, definitely marked by the underworld; my tabby became very anxious. He rushed to the window, his pink mouth wide open. . . . I let him in, and no sooner had he jumped on my lap than he relaxed, he went limp, not with fear, but happily, deliciously limp, and indicated by various signs known to me that he wanted his ears scratched — that done, he went to sleep.

We should learn to receive the love of God in silence and joy — that is what is meant by relaxing. He is always present, always giving us life, always round us and in us, like the air we breathe; there should be moments at least when we become more conscious of his presence: when we become conscious of it as the only reality, the one thing that will last for ever.[6]

Discussion Starters

1. How can favorite pets or other animals be reminders of God's presence in our lives?

2. What are your preferred ways of praying?

3. What do you feel you need to do to become more relaxed in God's presence?

4. What difference would it make in your life if you were more conscious of the presence of God as "the only reality, the one thing that will last for ever"?

Prayer Experience

1. Close your eyes. As you breathe deeply, image the air as a boundless ocean that surrounds you... as an ocean overflowing with the infinite love of God.... As you breathe in you are drawing in the fullness of divine love for you and for all creation.... As you breath out, image God's immense love flowing through you to your family, friends, co-workers, neighbors, strangers, the poor, the homeless, humanity, earth's creatures, pets, the entire universe.

2. Once you have relaxed in God's presence, read the reflection slowly and reflectively.

3. Be aware of how favorite pets or other animals remind you of God's loving presence. Reflect on how these creatures affect your thoughts, feelings, attitudes, and behavior. Imagine or observe your favorite animal with you now. Be present and playful with this animal in whatever way feels most natural to you. Contemplate and love this animal. Offer thanks for the gift of this favorite animal.

4. Reflect on your daily life. Become aware of times when God is inviting you to celebrate the divine presence in the ordinary events of your life such as a child's smile, a beautiful sunrise, a friend's tender kiss, a bird's song, a fragrant flower, a gentle rain, a melodious song, a relaxing bath, a delicious meal, an exhilarating jog. Make a list of these daily blessings. Choose one to experience in a deeper way. As you do so, be aware of any thoughts, feelings, insights, or images that emerge. Record these in poetry, dance, or in some other art form.

5. Take a walk in the woods, a park, or some favorite place. Imagine God is at your side, holding your hand as you walk. Enjoy the beauty of the earth. Allow the richness of creation to nourish you, embrace you, lift you up, fill you, renew you,

transform you. Become aware of your oneness with all earth's creatures and with God. Share your awe, wonder, and delight with God and with creation.

6. Be open to how your awareness of God's presence in your life can help you become more loving in your relationships with your family, friends, neighbors, faith community, and others. Decide on one concrete way you will live as a more loving person in your relationships with others now.

7. As you conclude your prayer reflection, close your eyes and let God possess you. Be conscious, as Caryll Houselander was, that God is always present, always giving you life, always around you and in you. Become aware that God's presence is "the only reality, the one thing that will last for ever."

Jessica Powers

(1905–1988)

Introduction

Jessica Powers was born on February 7, 1905, in Mauston, Wisconsin. Her parents, John and Delia Powers, were children of Irish immigrants. Jessica was the third of their four children. Her father died before Jessica began high school. After high school she studied journalism at Marquette University but quit after one year. She then worked as a secretary and wrote poetry. When her mother died, Jessica returned to help out on the farm. She stayed there until her brothers married. In 1937 she went to New York, where her first book of poetry, *The Lantern Burns,* was published in 1939.

In 1941 Jessica decided to become a contemplative and entered the Milwaukee Carmel. There she received a new name, Sister Miriam of the Holy Spirit. She made her perpetual vows in 1946, the year her second book of poems, *The Place of Splendor,* was published.

In 1955, 1958, and 1964, Jessica was elected prioress of her community. In 1958, she helped move her Carmel from Milwaukee to Pewaukee. These were busy years for Jessica, and she looked forward to a change: "I have been so busy being Martha that I have no Mary thoughts at all." When her term as prioress was almost over, she wrote, "My six-year term is up as Prioress, so there will necessarily be changes. I am so happy to have the good shelter of obedience again and to lead a life of simplicity — I was going to say, free from care, but who knows?"

Four books of poetry, *The Little Alphabet* (1955), *Mountain Sparrow* (1972), *Journey to Bethlehem* (1980), and *The House at Rest* (1984), preceded *Selected Poetry of Jessica Powers,* in which her poem "Pure Desert" is found. Jessica wrote close to four hundred poems and numerous letters, many of which are in private collections and in university archives.

In her poem "Pure Desert," Jessica describes the struggle a person might encounter in prayer. In an earlier letter she gives wise counsel on this painful spiritual experience: "In spite of the dealings I have had with souls, I know that it is difficult to discern what is a temporary sandstorm blinding one's vision, with clear blue air beyond, and what is hopeless desert waste which one will most likely succumb to, 'no way and no water' anywhere."[1]

Reflection

PURE DESERT

*"The more one runs in the spiritual life
the less tired one gets." — Padre Pio*

*This is pure Gobi desert, you declare;
I see, past sandstorms (of exaggeration)
and rage of flesh at ghostly motivation,
pink health invade your prayer.*

*Pure desert, you complain, though now you walk
who once had shuffled through the arid miles.
Sighting a day of flight, I shelve my smiles
and share your pilgrim talk.*

*All true ascesis as a desert lies:
hot wind, hot sand, no water and no way.
The ego agonizes through each day.
Freedom is when it dies.*

*I coax you onward: soon, first breeze of bliss;
soon, sun that scorches cooled to sun that warms.
Your youth will dance when shady lanes lock arms
with each green oasis.*[2]

Discussion Starters

1. Did you ever experience a time when prayer was difficult, when God seemed distant, when life was a struggle, when you felt emptiness, abandonment, desolation, "a desert time"? If so, how did you feel about this experience? If not, how would you respond if it happened now?

2. How does Jessica Powers's poem "Pure Desert" reflect your experience of prayer and the spiritual life?

3. How can encounters with God in "the desert" help us to grow spiritually? How can belonging to a faith or prayer community help us during "desert times"?

4. In what ways do you think the contemporary church is experiencing "the desert" in its struggles?

Prayer Experience

1. Sit in a comfortable position. Take several deep breaths. Let go of any outside noises or distractions. Relax and be still.

2. Read Jessica Powers's poem "True Desert" quietly, slowly.

3. Spend some time being with the images and metaphors of this poem. Select an image, metaphor, or symbol from the poem that touches you on a spiritual level. Ponder its richness and contemplate its meaning. Use this word, phrase, or metaphor as a mantra or centering prayer. Repeat it during your prayer time and throughout the day.

4. Reflect on one or more of your desert experiences, times when prayer was difficult, when God seemed distant, when life was a struggle, when you felt emptiness, abandonment, or desolation. Be aware of any feelings, thoughts, images, or insights that emerge.

5. Draw a symbol or a mandala of your desert experiences. You may wish to select classical or instrumental music that fits your reflection and use it for background prayer as you draw or paint your mandala or symbol.

6. During "desert times" picture yourself at the center of the mandala in God's loving presence or at the heart of the symbol with God. Allow the divine love to flow through you — liberating ... healing ... renewing ... energizing ... transforming ... filling you.

7. Read the story of God's chosen people in the desert in Exodus 16. The Israelites complained to Moses about the hardships of the desert: "If only we had died by the hand of the Lord in the land of Egypt, when we sat by the fleshpots and ate our fill, for you have brought us out into this wilderness to kill this whole assembly with hunger" (Exod. 16:3, NRSV). Dialogue with this text. Ask Moses and the Israelites to describe their desert experience and the growth that came from it. Share with a spiritual friend or faith community your insights into the desert experience of the Israelites and one or more of your own desert experiences. Invite your spiritual friend or faith community to share their insights into the desert experience of the Israelites and one or more of their own desert experiences with you. This communal sharing provides rich opportunities for expressing mutual support and encouragement in our journey through the desert experiences of our lives. You may wish to allow several sessions for this sharing.

Ita Ford

(1940–1980)

Introduction

Ita Ford was born in Brooklyn, New York, on April 23, 1940. She attended Catholic schools for twelve years. After graduating from Marymount Manhattan College with a B.A. in English, Ita entered the Maryknoll Sisters at twenty-one but left three years later when she was not accepted to profess vows. In 1971 she returned to Maryknoll and made a "promise of fidelity" in 1972. She worked as a missionary in Chile and in El Salvador until her death in 1980.

In August 1980, Ita and Maryknoll Sister Carla Piette were caught in a flash flood in El Salvador that overturned their jeep in a river. Carla, the driver, was able to push Ita out, but unfortunately did not survive herself. Reflecting on her own survival and grief and on the oppression and sufferings of the abandoned poor people of El Salvador, Ita expressed her commitment to new life in a letter to Jean Bauman, a friend:

> Carla's death and my not dying when I thought I would is a lot to absorb and takes time. I don't understand it, I don't like it — I have to humbly stand before the Lord and ask him to make sense of it since He's in charge. Meanwhile we keep plugging along because life is threatened by other evils worse than death — hatred, manipulation, vengeance, selfishness, etc. That's what we have to keep struggling against so that life-producing possibilities have a chance to flower.

During the 1970s and 1980s El Salvador experienced much economic, social, and political upheaval. Political and religious leaders who called for human rights, land reform, and justice for the poor were threatened, kidnapped, or murdered. People disappeared daily and were often later found tortured to death. Archbishop Oscar Romero, the Roman Catholic leader of El Salvador who spoke out for justice and peace in his land, was murdered as he celebrated Mass. On December 2, 1980, Ita Ford, Maryknoll Sister Maura Clarke, Ursuline Sister Dorothy Kazel, and missionary Jean Donovan were murdered by the National Guard on a deserted road at Hacienda San Francisco in El Salvador. According to news reports Ita was shot in the back of the head. As courageous witnesses to the dignity of the human person, the rights of the poor and destitute, the good news of the gospel, Ita Ford and these women, along with the thousands of others who died for the sake of the gospel in El Salvador, shine like bright stars in the darkness of night, reminding us, lest we forget, who we are called to be and who our God is — Doer of Justice, Seeker of Peace, and Liberator of the Oppressed.[1]

The following reflection is taken from a letter Ita wrote to her mother from El Salvador.

Reflection

I know this is a very hard time for you. I know that you're concerned and worried about the situation and I don't know really how to alleviate that. I truly believe that I should be here and I can't even tell you why. A couple of weeks ago Carla and I were praying and we both cried because it was so unclear to us why we were here, although we felt strongly we should be. Well, it's now quite clear for Carla, but I still have to keep asking to be shown. I can't tell you not to worry — that would be unnatural — it would be like someone saying to me — don't hurt because Carla died. In fact the last few days have been really hurting ones — probably because the shock of the whole thing — the event and to my system — is wearing off. All I can share with you is that God's palpable presence has never been more real ever since we came to Salvador — He's made a lot of things clear to us — what we should be doing, etc. — and I trust in that and I hope you can too.[2]

Discussion Starters

1. What impact did Ita Ford's recognition of the face of God incarnated in the poor and oppressed people of El Salvador have on her life and ministry?

2. In what ways are the poor people of the world seeking an end to the injustices that marginalize them and a respect for their human dignity as equal under God?

3. What can our contemporary society, swept up in materialism, learn from people like Ita Ford and the oppressed people of the world about the rich values of faith, culture, solidarity, community, trust, and generosity?

4. How can communities in which the people are empowered through faith, in which responsibility is shared, and in which the equality, gifts, and human dignity of all its members are affirmed enrich our vision of God, of the church, and of life?

Prayer Experience

1. Slowly take a few breaths. Be conscious of the air flowing through your nostrils as you breathe in and out. Be aware of places in your body where you feel stress or tension. Breathe relaxation into each of these areas... head, face, neck, shoulders, chest, upper back, arms, hands, fingers, abdomen, pelvis, lower back, legs, knees, ankles, feet, toes. Be still and rest in the embrace of the God of Compassion and Justice.

2. Read Ita Ford's letter to her mother slowly, prayerfully. Pause after each line to reflect on its meaning.

3. Reflect on ways you see the face of God incarnated in our world today in the poor, the homeless, the alienated, refugees, minorities, the elderly, people with handicaps, prisoners, drug addicts, people with AIDS, women. Record in your prayer journal any thoughts, insights, or images that arise from this reflection.

4. Pray for all victims of violence, injustice, oppression, discrimination, and hatred. Pray for all those who oppress, abuse,

discriminate, and hate others. Ask God to liberate and heal
the oppressed and their oppressors and bring peace and justice to our world. Pray that like Ita Ford you may be a doer of
justice, a seeker of peace, and a liberator of the oppressed.

5. Imagine yourself joining with others to courageously witness
   to the gospel values of human dignity, freedom, equality, and
   justice. In a prayerful dialogue, share with God your feelings,
   thoughts, insights, desires, hopes, and dreams about this ven-
   ture. Make a list of the possibilities. Examples: Commit your
   time, energy, talents, or money to groups who help the poor,
   single parents, families in crisis, the elderly, children at risk,
   people with disabilities, refugees, minorities. Join organizations
   that work for comprehensive health care, adequate housing,
   and good jobs for the unemployed, equality for women and
   minorities, environmental action. Join a peace and justice
   lobby such as Network, Bread for the World, or Greenpeace.
   Give to religious orders who work with the poor and oppressed
   people of the world or to relief organizations such as Catholic
   Charities, the Catholic Near East Welfare Society, or the Red
   Cross. Decide on one thing you will do to join with others in
   creating a more caring and just world.

6. Fast once a week for peace and justice in the world. Invite
   friends, neighbors, colleagues, or members of your faith community or church to join you. Donate the money saved to
   organizations that offer relief and work for justice and peace
   throughout the world.

7. Decide on one practical way you will simplify your lifestyle and
   use your resources to serve the poor. Examples: Donate food,
   clothing, furniture, tools, or children's toys that you no longer
   use or are willing to sacrifice to a charitable organization. Save
   money on processed food by planting a garden and donate the
   excess money and produce to a soup kitchen or shelter. Give
   homemade gifts for Christmas, birthdays, and anniversaries,
   and donate the money saved to the poor.

Rosa Parks

(b. 1913)

Introduction

Rosa Parks, the great granddaughter of slaves, was born in Tuskegee, Alabama, on February 4, 1913. Her father, James McCauley, was a carpenter and housebuilder. Rosa's mother, Leona Edwards, was a schoolteacher. Soon after Rosa was born, her family moved to Pine Level, Alabama, where they lived on Rosa's grandparents' farm. In 1915, when Rosa was two years old, her brother, Sylvester, was born. Soon afterward, their father left to find work, and Rosa did not see him very often during her childhood years.

As a little girl growing up in Alabama, Rosa hated the restrictions that African Americans experienced. "Jim Crow" laws kept black people and white people segregated. They were separated in churches, hotels, restaurants, theaters, buses, trains, parks, and other public places. Rosa knew it was wrong to judge people by the amount of money they earned, the clothes they wore, the homes they lived in, or the color of their skin. She grew up with a strong self-image and with pride in other African Americans. Rosa and her brother were taught by their mother, the only teacher, in a one-room school located in a small church. This school was open for five months a year. In Pine Level, school for black children ended after the sixth grade. Eleven-year-old Rosa continued her studies in a private school for black girls in Montgomery, Alabama. After graduating from junior high school, she took some high school courses at Alabama State College, which offered courses to students of all ages from nursery school through college. When Rosa was nineteen years old, she fell in love with Raymond Parks. Several weeks before her twentieth birthday, in December 1932, they got married in her home in Pine Level. Three years later, she graduated from high school.

Rosa worked first as a seamstress at her home, but later she found a job in the dressmaking department of a store. In the early 1940s, she joined the National Association for the Advancement of Colored People (NAACP), an organization that worked to get better houses and jobs for African Americans. As part of its mission, the NAACP sent lawyers into court to defend blacks who had been treated unfairly and worked to end the discrimination that African American and other minorities experienced.

Raymond Parks, Rosa's husband, had been a member of this organization. Soon after she joined, Rosa, an excellent typist and writer, became the secretary for the Alabama branch of the NAACP. This position enabled her to begin her work as a civil rights activist — writing letters, inviting speakers, arranging meetings, encouraging African Americans to vote. As a member of the Montgomery Voters League, an organization that worked for voting rights for black people, Rosa visited homes of African Americans and taught them what they needed to know to pass the voting test.

Rosa often walked the mile to and from work rather than take the bus. In Montgomery, where Rosa lived, the buses were segregated; blacks and whites were not permitted to sit together. If the white seats were filled and a white person got on the bus, the driver could tell a black person to stand so that the white person could sit down. Blacks were not permitted to walk through the white section of the bus. They had to pay their fare to the driver, then exit the bus and reenter through the back door. One day in 1943, Rosa decided to walk through the front section of the bus. Immediately, James Blake, the driver, ordered her to exit the bus and reenter through the back door. Before she could reenter, the bus drove away, leaving her at the bus stop without her fare.

December 1, 1955, was a day that started out like any other day for Rosa Parks, but a day in which her conscious choice changed the course of history for African Americans in this country and earned her the title "Mother of the Civil Rights Movement." Her courageous decision not to give up her bus seat to a white man and her arrest for breaking the city's segregation law were the first steps of the historic black civil rights movement. Rosa Parks's actions sparked the Montgomery bus boycott, and the efforts of thousands of others during the marches, demonstrations, sit-ins, and freedom rides that followed resulted in tremendous changes in our society. It is now illegal in the United States to discriminate against people because of their race, color, religion, or nationality in the workplace, hotels, restaurants, and other public places. All citizens may vote. Rosa Parks's commitment to racial equality is a prophetic challenge to all of us to keep on working for freedom, justice, and equality for people who suffer discrimination from racist and patriarchal structures, practices, policies, and systems throughout our world today.

Reflection

One evening in early December 1955, I was sitting in the front seat of the colored section of a bus in Montgomery, Alabama. The white people were sitting in the white section. More white people got on, and they filled up all the seats in the white section. When that happened, we black people were supposed to give up our seats to the whites. But I didn't move. The white driver said, "Let me have those front seats." I didn't get up. I was tired of giving in to white people.

"I'm going to have you arrested," the driver said.

"You may do that," I answered.

Two white policemen came. I asked one of them, "Why do you all push us around?"

He answered, "I don't know, but the law is the law and you're under arrest."[1]

"People always say that I didn't give up my seat because I was tired, but that isn't true. I was not tired physically.... No, the only tired I was, was tired of giving in."[2]

Discussion Starters

1. In what ways is Rosa Parks a mentor for today?

2. Have there been times that you experienced discrimination in your life because of race, gender, national origin, age, or disability? How did you respond to those situations?

3. Have there been times when you experienced or witnessed racial discrimination in your home? neighborhood? workplace? If so, how did you respond? If not, how would you respond if this occurred today?

4. How can you help to protect the civil rights of minorities in your local community? neighborhood? state? nation? church? world? In what ways can you work with others to transform racist and patriarchal structures, practices, policies, and systems in society?

Prayer Experience

1. Open yourself to the Spirit of God in your inner journey in one or more of the following ways: listen to gospel music, soul music, jazz, the blues; stand and sway, moan, sing, groan, cry, laugh, dance, and move to foot-stomping, soul-stirring music; beat a drum. Engage in these activities for as long as it takes to become aware of the liberating presence of God within you, within others, within the world.

2. Imagine the Rosa Parks bus incident as if you were present with her. Enter the bus with Rosa, watch her pay her fare, sit down, observe the white and black people on the bus, listen to the conversations between Rosa and the bus driver, the police officer, and others. Dialogue with Rosa. Ask her questions, listen to her answers, be attentive to her emotions, discover her strength, reflect on her insights; share your thoughts, feelings, emotions, and intuitions with her. Journey with her into the depths of racism, discrimination, and prejudice.

3. "No, the only tired I was, was tired of giving in." Become aware of the people in the world today who feel, like Rosa

Parks, battle-weary, exhausted, bruised from being discriminated against in our society. As each group, nation, or individual comes to mind, pray your own "psalm" as prayers of intercession for their deliverance, healing, and empowerment.

4. Share with God the times (if any) that you experienced discrimination in your life because of race, gender, national origin, age, or disability. Listen as God responds to your pain. Observe what God does to liberate, heal, and empower you. Offer forgiveness to the persons and/or institutions that discriminated against you. Decide on an appropriate response or action to ensure that this discrimination does not occur again.

5. Ask God for forgiveness for any times that you consciously or unconsciously discriminated against others or failed to support the victims of prejudice. Name each victim, ask for forgiveness, and receive forgiveness for each failure. Be aware of any changes in job, lifestyle, relationships, environment, etc., that you may need to make in order to live more justly, freely, equally, and responsibly with others as your sisters and brothers. Decide on one specific way you will do this.

6. Ask yourself this question: How can I help to protect the civil rights of minorities in my local community? neighborhood? state? nation? church? world? What difference might I make? Imagine God empowering you to work for justice and equality in these specific situations. See yourself sharing God's liberating, empowering love with the oppressed and their oppressors. Be aware of any new or deeper understandings of God, self, or others that you experienced.

7. Celebrate your experience of connectedness and bonding with Rosa Parks in some special way. One way of doing this is by starting a women's consciousness-raising group to reflect on one of the following: African American women's contributions in music, art, science, and politics; African American women's advocacy groups; African American women's efforts in education, research, health care, child care, housing, and politics.

Notes

—— 𝔜𝕮𝕺 ——

Introduction

1. Peter Dronke, *The Medieval Lyric* (New York: Harper and Row, 1969), 81.

2. Jos Van Mierlo, ed., *Hadewijch Brieven*, 2 vols. (Antwerp, 1947); cited in Ria Vanderauwera, "The Brabant Mystic Hadewijch," in Katharina M. Wilson, ed., *Medieval Women Writers* (Athens: University of Georgia Press, 1984), 200.

3. *Revelations de Sainte Mechtilde* (Tours, 1926), 11:393; cited in John A. Nichols and M. Thomas Shank, eds., *Peace Weavers*, Medieval Religious Women 2 (Kalamazoo, Mich.: Cistercian Publications, 1987), 218.

4. *Revelations of St. Gertrude*, chap. 61; cited in Phyllis Zagano, *Woman to Woman: An Anthology of Women's Spiritualities* (Collegeville, Minn.: Liturgical Press, 1993), 13–14.

5. Mrs. George Ripley, trans., *Life and Doctrine of Saint Catherine of Genoa* 40 (New York: Christian Press Association Publishing, 1896); cited in Carol Lee Flinders, *Enduring Grace* (San Francisco: Harper and Row, 1993), 130.

6. Marguerite d'Oingt, *Pagina Meditationum*, chaps. 30–39, *Oeuvres*, 77–79; cited in Caroline Walker Bynum, *Jesus as Mother* (Berkeley: University of California Press, 1982), 153.

7. Edmund Colledge and James Walsh, trans., *Julian of Norwich: Showings* (New York: Paulist, 1978), 293–95.

8. Zagano, *Woman to Woman*, 46–47.

9. Joan Chittister, "Religious Life Is Still Alive but Far from Promised Land," *National Catholic Reporter*, February 18, 1994.

10. Zagano, *Woman to Woman*, 54–55.

11. *The Story of a Soul: The Autobiography of St. Thérèse of Lisieux*, trans. John Clarke, O.C.D. (Washington, D.C.: Institute of Carmelite Studies, 1972). Quotations taken from this source are cited in the text using the abbreviation *Story*.

12. *Evelyn Underhill on Prayer*, ed. Tony Castle (London: Marshall Pickering, 1989), 41–42.

13. *Selected Poetry of Jessica Powers*, ed. Regina Siegfried and Robert Morneau (Kansas City: Sheed and Ward, 1989); cited in Zagano, *Woman to Woman*, 93.

14. Zagano, *Woman to Woman*, 107.

15. Teresa Gelsi, *Rosa Parks and the Montgomery Bus Boycott* (Brookfield, Conn.: Millbrook Press, 1991), 16.

Perpetua

1. *Acts of Perpetua and Felicitas* 10, trans. H. Musurillo, in *The Acts of the Christian Martyrs* (Oxford: Clarendon, 1972), 107–31; cited in Barbara Bowie, Kathleen Hughes, Sharon Karam, and Carolyn Osiek, eds., *Silent Voices, Sacred Lives* (New York: Paulist, 1992), 365–66.
2. *Acts of Perpetua* 21; cited in Bowie, *Silent Voices*, 371.
3. *Acts of Perpetua* 2–3; cited in Bowie, *Silent Voices*, 359–60.

Irene

1. *Martyrdom of Saints Agape, Irene, Chione, and Companions at Thessalonica* 1–2, trans. H. Musurillo, in *The Acts of the Christian Martyrs* (Oxford: Clarendon, 1972), 281–93; cited in Barbara Bowie, Kathleen Hughes, Sharon Karam, and Carolyn Osiek, eds., *Silent Voices, Sacred Lives* (New York: Paulist, 1992), 405–6.
2. *Martyrdom at Thessalonica* 6; cited in Bowie, *Silent Voices*, 411–12.
3. *Martyrdom at Thessalonica* 5; cited in Bowie, *Silent Voices*, 409–10.

Desert Mother Sarah

1. *Sayings of the Desert Mothers Sarah, Syncletica, and Theodora*, trans. Benedicta Ward, in *The Desert Christian: Sayings of the Desert Fathers; The Alphabetical Collection* (New York: Macmillan, 1975), 229–30; cited in Barbara Bowie, Kathleen Hughes, Sharon Karam, and Carolyn Osiek, eds., *Silent Voices, Sacred Lives* (New York: Paulist, 1992), 458–59.
2. Ward, *Sayings*, 229–30; cited in Bowie, *Silent Voices*, 392.

Desert Mother Theodora

1. Benedicta Ward, *The Desert Christian: Sayings of the Desert Fathers; The Alphabetical Collection* (New York: Macmillan, 1975), 82–84, 229–35; cited in Barbara Bowie, Kathleen Hughes, Sharon Karam, and Carolyn Osiek, eds., *Silent Voices, Sacred Lives* (New York: Paulist, 1992), 199.
2. Cassian, a prominent desert monk, defines *accidie* as a state of inner turmoil.
3. Ward, *The Desert Christian*, 83, 229–35; cited in Bowie, *Silent Voices*, 199–200.

Desert Mother Syncletica

1. Benedicta Ward, *The Desert Christian: Sayings of the Desert Fathers; The Alphabetical Collection* (New York: Macmillan, 1975), 235, 232, 231; cited in Barbara Bowie, Kathleen Hughes, Sharon Karam, and Carolyn Osiek, eds., *Silent Voices, Sacred Lives* (New York: Paulist, 1992), 102.

2. Ward, *The Desert Christian*, 234; cited in Bowie, *Silent Voices*, 101.

Paula

1. Jerome, *Life of Paula*, 3, *Letters*, ed. Philip Schaat, ser. 2, vol. 6 (Grand Rapids: William B. Eerdmans, 1952), 157–63, 195–212, 253–8; cited in Barbara Bowie, Kathleen Hughes, Sharon Karam, and Carolyn Osiek, eds., *Silent Voices, Sacred Lives* (New York: Paulist, 1992), 179–80.

2. Jerome, *Life of Paula*, 15–16; cited in Bowie, *Silent Voices*, 181.

3. Jerome, *Life of Paula*, 27; cited in Bowie, *Silent Voices*, 187.

4. Jerome, *Life of Paula*, 28–29; cited in Bowie, *Silent Voices*, 188.

5. Jerome, *Life of Paula*, 27–29, 30–31; cited in Bowie, *Silent Voices*, 189–90.

6. Jerome, *Life of Paula*, 28–29; cited in Bowie, *Silent Voices*, 188.

Dhuoda

1. James Manchand, "The Frankish Mother Dhuoda," in Katharina M. Wilson, ed., *Medieval Women Writers* (Athens: University of Georgia Press, 1984), 1.

2. Ibid., 4.

3. Ibid., 25–26.

4. Ibid., 12.

5. Ibid., 16.

Hildegard of Bingen

1. Barbara Newman, "Divine Power Made Perfect in Weakness," in John A. Nichols and M. Thomas Shank, eds., *Peace Weavers*, Medieval Religious Women 2 (Kalamazoo, Mich.: Cistercian Publications, 1987), 104.

2. Bernhard W. Scholz, "Hildegard Von Bingen on the Nature of Woman," *American Benedictine Review* (1980): 370f.

3. Newman, "Divine Power," 105.

4. Hildegard von Bingen, *Scivias* 111.11; Adelgundis Fuhrkotter, ed., *Das Leben der bl. Hildegard von Bingen* (Dusseldorf, 1968), 586.

5. Ibid., 112.

6. Pope John Paul II, "Pope's Letter to Cardinal Volk, Bishop of Mainz," *L'Osservatore Romano*, October 1, 1979, 10.

7. This illumination is the fourth vision in *De Operatione Dei*, entitled "On the Articulation of the Body," 79–184, 83f; *Illuminations of Hildegard of Bingen*, trans. Matthew Fox (Santa Fe: Bear & Company, 1985), 47–48.

8. Ibid., 47.

Beatrice of Nazareth

1. Phyllis Zagano, *Woman to Woman: An Anthology of Women's Spiritualities* (Collegeville, Minn.: Liturgical Press, 1993), 8–9.

2. Beatrice of Nazareth, *The Seven Steps of Love*, trans. Mary Josepha Carton, B.V.M., Cistercian Studies 19, no. 1 (1984); cited in ibid., 10.

Hadewijch of Brabant

1. *Hadewijch: The Complete Works*, trans. and introduction Columba Hart, O.S.B. (New York: Paulist, 1980), 5.

2. N. de Paepe, *Hadewijch: Strofische Gedichten*; cited in Ria Vanderauwera, "The Brabant Mystic Hadewijch," in Katharina M. Wilson, ed., *Medieval Women Writers* (Athens: University of Georgia Press, 1984), 187–88.

3. Jos Van Mierlo, ed., *Hadewijch Brieven*, 2 vols. (Antwerp, 1947), 2:200–201.

4. *Hadewijch: The Complete Works*, 272.

Mechtild of Magdeburg

1. Edith Scholl, "To Be a Full-Grown Bride: Mechtild of Magdeburg," in John A. Nichols and M. Thomas Shank, eds., *Peace Weavers*, Medieval Religious Women 2 (Kalamazoo, Mich.: Cistercian Publications, 1987), 223. All quotations are taken from the Lucy Menzies translation, *The Revelation of Mechtild of Magdeburg* (London: Longmans, Green and Co., 1953), and are cited by book and chapter.

2. Sue Woodruff, *Meditations with Mechtild of Magdeburg* (Santa Fe: Bear & Company, 1982), 92, 95.

Mechtild of Hackeborn

1. Jeremy Finnegan, "Saint Mechtild of Hackeborn: Nemo Communior," in John A. Nichols and M. Thomas Shank, eds., *Peace Weavers*, Medieval Religious Women 2 (Kalamazoo, Mich.: Cistercian Publications, 1987), 214.

2. *Revelationes Gertrudianae ac Mechtildianae*, ed. Dom Ludwig Paquelin (Paris, 1875–77), 35:286; cited in Finnegan, "Saint Mechtild," 215.

3. *Revelations de Sainte Mechtilde* (Tours: 1926), 11:261; cited in Finnegan, "Saint Mechtild," 216.

4. *Revelations de Sainte Mechtilde*, 50:296; cited in Finnegan, "Saint Mechtild," 218.

5. *Revelations de Sainte Mechtilde*, 32:284; cited in Finnegan, "Saint Mechtild," 218.

6. *Revelations de Sainte Mechtilde*, 35:235; cited in Finnegan, "Saint Mechtild," 218.

7. *Revelations de Sainte Mechtilde*; cited in Finnegan, "Saint Mechtild," 218.

8. Finnegan, "Saint Mechtild," 211.

9. *Revelationes Gertrudianae*, 15:208; cited in Finnegan, "Saint Mechtild," 217.

10. *Revelationes Gertrudianae*, 27:225; cited in Finnegan, "Saint Mechtild," 217.

11. *Revelationes Gertrudianae*, 6:256; cited in Finnegan, "Saint Mechtild," 217.

Gertrude the Great

1. Gertrude the Great, *The Herald of God's Loving Kindness*, trans. Alexandra Barrat (Kalamazoo, Mich.: Cistercian Publications, 1991); cited in M. Thomas Shank, "The God of My Life: St. Gertrude, A Monastic Woman," in John A. Nichols and M. Thomas Shank, eds., *Peace Weavers*, Medieval Religious Women 2 (Kalamazoo, Mich.: Cistercian Publications, 1987), 239.

2. *Revelations of St. Gertrude*, chap. 61; cited in Phyllis Zagano, *Woman to Woman: An Anthology of Women's Spiritualities* (Collegeville, Minn.: Liturgical Press, 1993), 13–14.

3. *Revelations of St. Gertrude*, chap. 61; cited in Zagano, *Woman to Woman*, 12–13.

4. *Revelations of St. Gertrude*, chap. 61; cited in Zagano, *Woman to Woman*, 14–15.

Clare of Assisi

1. Carol Lee Flinders, *Enduring Grace* (San Francisco: Harper and Row, 1993), 19.

2. Regis J. Armstrong, O.F.M., ed. and trans., *Early Documents*, 2.40 (New York: Paulist, 1988); cited in Flinders, *Enduring Grace*, 23.

3. First Letter, no. 25, in Armstrong, 193; cited in Madge Karecki, "Clare: Poverty and Contemplation," in John A. Nichols and M. Thomas Shank, eds.,

Peace Weavers, Medieval Religious Women 2 (Kalamazoo, Mich.: Cistercian Publications, 1987), 169, 171.

4. First Letter, nos. 15–17, in Armstrong, 192; cited in Karecki, "Clare: Poverty," 173.

5. Ignatius Brady, ed., *The Legend and Writings of St. Clare of Assisi* (St. Bonaventure, N.Y.: Franciscan Institute, 1953), 75; cited in Karecki, "Clare: Poverty," 171.

6. Brady, *Legend and Writings,* 129–30; cited in Karecki, "Clare: Poverty," 171.

7. Armstrong, *Early Documents,* 44; cited in Flinders, *Enduring Grace,* 23.

Angela of Foligno

1. *The Divine Consolation of the Blessed Angela of Foligno,* trans. Mary G. Steegman (London, 1909), 19; cited in Lucy Menzies, *Mirrors of the Holy* (Oxford: A. R. Mowbray & Company, 1928), 57.

2. *Divine Consolation,* 1; cited in Menzies, *Mirrors,* 61.

3. *Divine Consolation,* 5; cited in Menzies, *Mirrors,* 64–65.

4. *Divine Consolation;* cited in Menzies, *Mirrors,* 80.

5. *Divine Consolation,* 259; cited in Menzies, *Mirrors,* 89.

6. Menzies, *Mirrors,* 138.

Catherine of Siena

1. *The Dialogue,* trans. Suzanne Noffke, 100 (New York: Paulist, 1980); cited in Phyllis Zagano, *Woman to Woman: An Anthology of Women's Spiritualities* (Collegeville, Minn.: Liturgical Press, 1993), 34.

2. Zagano, *Woman to Woman,* 25–26.

3. Lucy Menzies, *Mirrors of the Holy* (Oxford: A. R. Mowbray & Company, 1928), 138.

Catherine of Genoa

1. Mrs. George Ripley, trans., *Life and Doctrine of Saint Catherine of Genoa* 40 (New York: Christian Press Association Publishing, 1896); cited in Carol Lee Flinders, *Enduring Grace* (San Francisco: Harper and Row, 1993), 129–33. Quotations taken from this source are cited in the text using the abbreviation *Life.*

2. Catherine of Genoa, *Purgation and Purgatory, Spiritual Dialogue,* trans. Serge Hughes (New York: Paulist, 1979), 130; cited in Flinders, *Enduring Grace,* 141.

Marguerite d'Oingt

1. Elizabeth Alvilda Petroff, "Women, Heresy, and Holiness in Early Fourteenth-Century France," *Medieval Women's Visionary Literature* (Oxford: Oxford University Press, 1986), 278, 280.

2. Petroff, Introduction to *Medieval Women*, 43–44.

3. Petroff, "Women, Heresy, and Holiness," 278.

4. Ibid., 278–79.

5. Marguerite d'Oingt, *Pagina Meditationum*, chaps. 30–39, *Oeuvres*, 77–79; cited in Caroline Walker Bynum, *Jesus as Mother* (Berkeley: University of California Press, 1982), 153.

Julian of Norwich

1. Gloria Durka, *Praying with Julian of Norwich* (Winona, Minn.: St. Mary's Press, 1989), 15.

2. Source of both Merton quotes: Thomas Merton, *Confessions of a Guilty Bystander*, as quoted in *Julian of Norwich: Four Studies to Commemorate the Sixth Centenary of the Revelations of Divine Love* (Oxford: Fairacres Press, 1975), 37.

3. *Julian of Norwich: Showings*, trans. Edmund Colledge, O.S.A., and James Walsh, S.J., Classics of Western Spirituality (New York: Paulist, 1978), 293–95.

Teresa of Avila

1. Teresa of Avila, *Autobiography*; cited in Sister Mary, O.D.C., *Daily Readings with St. Teresa of Avila* (Springfield, Ill.: Templegate Publishers, 1985), 11.

2. Sister Mary, *Daily Readings with St. Teresa of Avila*, 11–12.

3. Ibid., 13.

4. Ibid., 14.

5. Carol Lee Flinders, *Enduring Grace* (San Francisco: Harper and Row, 1993), 170–71.

6. Teresa of Avila, "The Fourth Dwelling Places," *The Interior Castle*, chap. 3, trans. Kieran Kavanaugh and Otilio Rodriguez (New York: Paulist, 1979); cited in Zagano, *Woman to Woman*, 43.

Jane Frances de Chantal

1. Phyllis Zagano, *Woman to Woman: An Anthology of Women's Spiritualities* (Collegeville, Minn.: Liturgical Press, 1993), 46–47.

2. Wendy M. Wright, "Two Faces of Christ: Jeanne de Chantal," in John A. Nichols and M. Thomas Shank, eds., *Peace Weavers*, Medieval Religious Women 2 (Kalamazoo, Mich.: Cistercian Publications, 1987), 355.

3. *Francis de Sales, Jane de Chantal: Letters of Spiritual Direction*, introduction by Wendy M. Wright and Joseph F. Power, O.S.F.S., Classics of Western Spirituality (Mahwah, N.J.: Paulist, 1986), 202–3.

Mary Ward

1. Mary Ward, Letter to the apostolic nuncio of Lower Germany, Monsignor Albergato, 1620 (found in the Institute Archives in Munich [AIM]); cited in Phyllis Zagano, *Woman to Woman: An Anthology of Women's Spiritualities* (Collegeville, Minn.: Liturgical Press, 1993), 58.

2. Mary Ward, AIM Various Papers, no. 10 (found in the Institute Archives in Munich [AIM]); cited in Zagano, *Woman to Woman*, 60.

3. Zagano, *Woman to Woman*, 54–55.

4. M. Emmanuel Orchard, I.B.V.M, ed., *Till God Will: Mary Ward through Her Writings* (London: Darton, Longman and Todd, 1985), 57, 58.

Elizabeth Bayley Seton

1. Elizabeth Bayley Seton, *Journal*, March 25, 1805; cited in Phyllis Zagano, *Woman to Woman: An Anthology of Women's Spiritualities* (Collegeville, Minn.: Liturgical Press, 1993), 72.

2. Zagano, *Woman to Woman*, 70–71.

3. Seton, *Journal*, approx. 1809; cited in Zagano, *Woman to Woman*, 73.

Thérèse of Lisieux

1. Ida Gorres, *The Hidden Face: A Study of St. Thérèse of Lisieux* (New York: Pantheon, 1959), 27.

2. *The Story of a Soul: The Autobiography of St. Thérèse of Lisieux*, trans. John Clarke, O.C.D. (Washington, D.C.: Institute of Carmelite Studies, 1972). Quotations taken from this source are cited in the text using the abbreviation *Story*.

3. Thérèse of Lisieux, *Collected Letters* (London: Sheed and Ward, 1949), 292.

Evelyn Underhill

1. Margaret Cropper, *Evelyn Underhill* (London: Longmans, Green and Company, 1958), 5.

2. Ibid., 2.

3. Ibid., 30.

4. Evelyn Underhill, "Mysticism and Magic," *Mysticism;* cited in Cropper, *Evelyn Underhill,* 45.

5. Cropper, *Evelyn Underhill,* 10.

6. *Evelyn Underhill on Prayer,* ed. Tony Castle (London: Marshall Pickering, 1989), 41–42.

Edith Stein

1. Phyllis Zagano, *Woman to Woman: An Anthology of Women's Spiritualities* (Collegeville, Minn.: Liturgical Press, 1993), 76–77.

2. Ibid., 78.

3. *The Collected Works of Edith Stein, Sister Benedicta of the Cross, Discalced Carmelite,* trans. Freda Mary Oben (Washington, D.C.: ICS Publications, 1987), 2:86–87.

Dorothy Day

1. Phyllis Zagano, *Woman to Woman: An Anthology of Women's Spiritualities* (Collegeville, Minn.: Liturgical Press, 1993), 83.

2. Ibid., 82–83.

3. Dorothy Day, *Loaves and Fishes* (San Francisco: Harper & Row, 1983); cited in Zagano, *Woman to Woman,* 84.

4. Day, *Loaves and Fishes;* cited in Zagano, *Woman to Woman,* 85.

5. Day *Loaves and Fishes;* cited in Zagano, *Woman to Woman,* 86.

6. Zagano, *Woman to Woman,* 87–88.

Caryll Houselander

1. Caryll Houselander, *A Rocking Horse Catholic* (Westminster, Md.: Christian Classics, 1988), 3, 26.

2. Ibid., 30, 34.

3. Ibid., 45–47.

4. Ibid., 68–69.

5. Ibid., 134–35.

6. Caryll Houselander, *The Comforting of Christ* (London: Sheed and Ward, 1947), 14–15.

Jessica Powers

1. Phyllis Zagano, *Woman to Woman: An Anthology of Women's Spiritualities* (Collegeville, Minn.: Liturgical Press, 1993), 90. Background information for

Jessica Powers is found on pp. 89–90; letter selections are taken from Margaret Ellen Traxler, S.S.N.D., papers.

2. *Selected Poetry of Jessica Powers*, ed. Regina Siegfried and Robert Morneau (Kansas City: Sheed & Ward, 1989); cited in Zagano, *Woman to Woman*, 93.

Ita Ford

1. Phyllis Zagano, *Woman to Woman: An Anthology of Women's Spiritualities* (Collegeville, Minn.: Liturgical Press, 1993), 104–5.

2. Ibid., 107.

Rosa Parks

1. Rosa Parks with Jim Haskins, *Rosa Parks: My Story* (New York: Dial Books, 1992), 1.

2. Ibid., 116.

Resources for Praying with Passionate Women

Martyrdom of Perpetua and Irene

Acts of Perpetua and Felicitas. Translated by H. Musurillo in *The Acts of the Christian Martyrs*. Oxford: Clarendon, 1972, pp. 107–31.

Martyrdom of Saints Agape, Irene, Chione and Companions at Thessalonica. Translated by J. Musurillo in *The Acts of the Christian Martyrs*. Oxford: Clarendon, 1972, pp. 281–93.

Sayings of the Desert Mothers Sarah, Theodora, and Syncletica

The Desert Christian: Sayings of the Desert Fathers; The Alphabetical Collection. Translated by Benedicta Ward. New York: Macmillan, 1975, pp. 82–84, 229–35.

Dhuoda

Dhuoda, On John 15 to Her Son. Translation and Introduction by Morsel Thiebaux. New York: Garland Publishing Company, 1987.

Beatrice of Nazareth

The Seven Steps of Love. Translated by Mary Josepha Carton, B.V.M. Cistercian Studies 19, no. 1 (1984).

Hadewijch of Brabant

Hadewijch: The Complete Works. Translation and introduction by Mother Columba Hart, O.S.B. New York: Paulist, 1980.

Hildegard of Bingen

Hildegard of Bingen. Translation and introduction by Marcelle Thiebaux. The Writings of Medieval Women. New York: Garland Publishing Company, 1987.

Hildegard of Bingen: Scivias. Translated by Columba Hart and Jane Bishop. New York: Paulist, 1990.

Mechtild of Magdeburg

The Revelations of Mechtild of Magdeburg, or The Flowing Light of the Godhead. Translated by Lucy Menzies. London: Longmans, Green, 1953.

Mechtild von Magdeburg, Flowing Light of the Divinity. Translated by Christiane Mesch Galvani, edited and with an introduction by Susan Clark. New York: Garland Publishing, 1991.

Woodruff, Sue. *Meditations with Mechtild of Magdeburg.* Santa Fe, N.M.: Bear & Co., 1982.

Gertrude the Great

"Spiritual Exercises," in *The Fire and the Cloud: An Anthology of Catholic Spirituality.* Edited by David Fleming. New York: Paulist, 1978.

Love, Peace, and Joy: A Month of the Sacred Heart according to St. Gertrude. Translated by Andre Prevot. Hales Corners, Wisc.: Sacred Heart Monastery, 1911.

Clare of Assisi

Early Documents. Edited and translated by Regis J. Armstrong, O.F.M. Cap. New York: Paulist, 1988.

Francis and Clare: The Complete Works. Edited by Regis J. Armstrong and Ignatius C. Brady. New York: Paulist, 1982.

Angela of Foligno

Menzies, Lucy. *Mirrors of the Holy.* London: A. R. Mowbray & Company, 1928.

Catherine of Siena

Catherine of Siena: Dialogue. Translation and introduction by Suzanne Noffke, O.P. New York: Paulist, 1980.

The Letters of Catherine of Siena. Translated by Suzanne Noffke. Binghamton: Center for Medieval and Early Renaissance Studies, State University of New York, 1988.

Catherine of Genoa

Purgation and Purgatory, the Spiritual Dialogue. Translated by Serge Hughes. New York: Paulist, 1979.

Life and Doctrine of Saint Catherine of Genoa. Translated by Mrs. George Ripley. New York: Christian Press Association Publishing, 1896.

Julian of Norwich

Julian of Norwich: Showings. Translated by Edmund Colledge, O.S.A. and James Walsh, S.J. New York: Paulist, 1978.

Julian of Norwich: An Introductory Appreciation and an Interpretative Anthology. Edited by P. Franklin Chambers. London: Gollancz, 1955.

Teresa of Avila

The Collected Works of St. Teresa of Avila. Translated by Kieran Kavanaugh and Otilio Rodriguez. Washington: Institute for Carmelite Studies, 1976.

The Interior Castle. Translated by Kieran Kavanaugh and Otilio Rodriguez. New York: Paulist, 1979.

The Life of Teresa of Jesus: The Autobiography of St. Teresa of Avila. Edited and translated by E. Allison Peers. Garden City: Image Books, 1960.

Jane Frances de Chantal

Saint Jane Frances Frémyot de Chantal: Her Exhortations, Conferences and Instructions. Chicago: Loyola University Press, 1928.

Selected Letters of Saint Jane Frances de Chantal. Translated by Sisters of the Visitation, Harrow-on-the-Hill. London: R & T Washburn, 1918.

Mary Ward

Till God Will: Mary Ward through Her Writings. Edited by Emmanuel Orchard, I.B.V.M. London: Darton, Longman and Todd, 1985.

Byrne, Lavinia, ed. *The Hidden Tradition: Women's Spiritual Writings Rediscovered.* New York: Crossroad, 1991.

Elizabeth Seton

Elizabeth Seton: Selected Writings. Edited by Ellin M. Kelly and Annabelle M. Melville. New York: Paulist, 1987.

Letters of Mother Seton to Mrs. Julianna Scott. Edited by Joseph B. Code. New York: Father Salvator M. Burgio Memorial Foundation in Honor of Mother Seton, 1960.

Thérèse of Lisieux

The Story of a Soul: The Autobiography of St. Thérèse of Lisieux. Translated by John Clarke, O.C.D. Washington, D.C.: Institute of Carmelite Studies, 1972.

Thérèse of Lisieux: Her Last Conversations. Translated by John Clarke, O.C.D. Washington, D.C.: Institute of Carmelite Studies, 1977.

Evelyn Underhill

Cropper, Margaret. *Evelyn Underhill.* London: Longmans, Green and Company, 1958.

Evelyn Underhill on Prayer. Edited by Tony Castle. London: Marshall Pickering, 1989.

Edith Stein

Essays on Women. Edited by L. Gelber and Romaeus Leuven. Translated by Freda Mary Ubren. Washington: ICS Publications, 1986.

On the Problem of Empathy. Translated by Waltraut Stein. The Hague: M. Nijhoff, 1964.

Writings Selected. Translated and introduced by Hilda Graef. Westminster, Md.: Newman Press, 1956.

Dorothy Day

By Little and by Little: The Selected Writings of Dorothy Day. Edited by Robert Ellsberg. New York: Knopf, 1983.

House of Hospitality. New York: Sheed & Ward, 1939.

Loaves and Fishes. San Francisco: Harper & Row, 1983.

The Long Loneliness: The Autobiography of Dorothy Day. San Francisco: Harper & Row, 1952.

Caryll Houselander

A Rocking Horse Catholic. Westminster, Md.: Christian Classics, 1988.

Jessica Powers

The Lantern Burns. New York: Monastire Press, 1939.

Selected Poetry of Jessica Powers. Edited by Regina Siegfried and Robert Morneau. Kansas City: Sheed & Ward, 1989.

Leckey, Dolores. *Winter Music: A Life of Jessica Powers Poet, Nun, Woman of the 20th Century.* Kansas City: Sheed & Ward, 1993.

Ita Ford

Brett, D. W., and E. T. Brett. *Murdered in Central America: The Stories of Eleven U.S. Missionaries.* Maryknoll, N.Y.: Orbis Books, 1988.

Noone, Judith M., M.M. *Same Fate as the Poor.* Maryknoll, N.Y.: Maryknoll Sisters of St. Dominic, 1984. Ita Ford's writings have been collected by Judith Noone, M.M. for *Same Fate as the Poor,* and are located in the Maryknoll Archives.

Rosa Parks

Adler, David A. *A Picture Book of Rosa Parks.* New York: Holiday House, 1993.

Celsi, Teresa. *Rosa Parks and the Montgomery Bus Boycott.* Brookfield, Conn.: Millbrook Press, 1991.

Greenfield, Eloise. *Rosa Parks.* New York: Harper Collins, 1973.

Parks, Rosa with Jim Haskins. *Rosa Parks: My Story.* New York: Dial Books, 1992.

BOOKS ON WOMEN MYSTICS

Bowie, Barbara, Kathleen Hughes, Sharon Karam, and Carolyn Osiek, eds. *Silent Voices, Sacred Lives: Women's Readings for the Liturgical Year.* New York: Paulist, 1992. This book provides a rich array of readings for the liturgical year. I was profoundly touched and enriched by the accounts of Perpetua and Irene's martyrdom, the sayings of the desert mothers Sarah, Theodora, and Syncletica, and the Life of Paula. These accounts as well as others give us the image of women no longer silent in the church. We can use the inclusive, rich resource for inclusive worship in our communities.

Bynum, Caroline Walker. *Jesus as Mother.* Berkeley: University of California Press, 1982. A collection of scholarly essays introducing readers to the use of feminine imagery in medieval piety. Bynum introduces us to mystics who address Jesus as mother in this era.

——. *Holy Feast and Holy Fast: The Religious Significance of Food to Medieval Women.* Berkeley and Los Angeles: University of California Press, 1987. An interesting presentation of the food practices of medieval women.

Flinders, Carol Lee. *Enduring Grace.* San Francisco: Harper, 1993. From Clare of Assisi in the Middle Ages to Thérèse of Lisieux in the nineteenth century, Carol Lee Flinders reveals compelling portraits of seven women mystics. Excellent for reflection, meditation, and group discussion.

Nichols, John A., and M. Thomas Shank, eds. *Distant Echoes.* Medieval Religious Women 1. Kalmazoo, Mich.: Cistercian Publications, 1984. This broad anthology presents essays on the lives and circumstances of medieval religious women. Among the topics included are "Lives of Consecrated Women in the Fourth Century," "Feminine Lay Piety in the High Middle Ages: The Beguines," and "Medieval Cistercian Nunneries and English Bishops."

Nichols, John A., and M. Thomas Shank, eds. *Peace Weavers.* Medieval Religious Women 2. Kalmazoo, Mich.: Cistercian Publications, 1987. Powerful essays by twenty-four scholars on mystics such as Clare of Assisi, Mechtild of Hackeborn, Mechtild of Magdeburg, Gertrude the Great, Catherine of Siena, Julian of Norwich, Teresa of Avila, and Jane de Chantal.

Petroff, Elizabeth Alvilda. *Medieval Women's Visionary Literature.* New York: Oxford University Press, 1986. Excellent general introduction on the visionary tradition of women's writing. Excerpts included on women in the early church (Perpetua and Macrina) and medieval mystics (Hadewijch, Beatrice of Nazareth, Mechtild of Magdeburg, Gertrude the Great, Clare of Assisi, Angela of Foligno, Catherine of Siena, Marguerite d'Oingt, and Julian of Norwich).

Wilson, Katharina M., ed. *Medieval Women Writers.* Athens: University of Georgia Press, 1984. This scholarly anthology contains writings of fifteen women who span seven centuries, eight languages, and ten regions. Some of the writers included are Dhuoda, Heloise, Hildegard of Bingen, Mechtild of Magdeburg, Hadewijch, Bridget of Sweden, Catherine of Siena, Julian of Norwich, and Margery Kempe.

Zagano, Phyllis. *Woman to Woman: An Anthology of Women's Spiritualities.* Collegeville, Minn.: Liturgical Press, 1993. A superb book for prayerful contemplation of the following women: Hildegard of Bingen, Beatrice of Nazareth, Gertrude the Great, Julian of Norwich, Catherine of Siena, Teresa of Avila, Jane Frances de Chantal, Mary Ward, Jeanne Marie Guyon, Elizabeth Seton, Edith Stein, Dorothy Day, Jessica Powers, Simone Weil, and Ita Ford. From my reflection on these and other women came the vision of *Praying with Passionate Women.*